Also in the Children's Television Workshop
Family Living Series

Parents' Guide to Raising Kids Who Love to Learn:
Infant to Grade School

Parents' Guide to Feeding Your Kids Right:
Birth Through Teen Years

FAMILY LIVING SERIES™

Parents' Guide to

Understanding Discipline

Infancy Through Preteen

• • • • • • • • • • • • • •

CHILDREN'S TELEVISION WORKSHOP

Written by Mary Lee Grisanti,
Dian G. Smith,
and Charles Flatter, Ph.D.

Preface by Lawrence Balter, Ph.D.

PRENTICE
HALL
PRESS

• • • • • • • • • • • • • •

New York • London • Toronto • Sydney
• Tokyo • Singapore

Note: Chapter Seven was adapted from two articles (''When Kids Get Angry'' and ''When Parents Get Angry'') by Helen Geraghty, which appeared in the *Sesame Street Magazine Parents' Guide* and the *Sesame Street Parents' Newsletter.*

CHILDREN'S TELEVISION WORKSHOP
Chairman—Chief Executive Officer: Joan Ganz Cooney
President: David Britt
Publisher: Nina Link

Series Editor: Marge Kennedy
Senior Editor: Sima Bernstein
Child Development Consultant: Istar Schwager, Ph.D.
Writers: Mary Lee Grisanti, Dian G. Smith, and Charles Flatter, Ph.D.

 PRENTICE HALL PRESS
15 Columbus Circle
New York, NY 10023

Library of Congress Cataloging-in-Publication Data

Grisanti, Mary Lee.
    Parent's guide to understanding discipline ; infancy through preteen / Children's Television Workshop ; written by Mary Lee Grisanti, Dian G. Smith & Charles Flatter ; preface by Lawrence Balter.—1st ed.
        p.   cm.—(Children's Television Workshop family living series)
    Includes bibliographical references.
    ISBN 0-13-649997-X : $9.95
    1. Discipline in children. 2. Parent and child. 3. Child rearing. I. Smith, Dian G. II. Flatter, Charles. III. Children's Television Workshop. IV. Title. V. Series.
HQ770.4.G75   1990
649'.64—dc20   89-71007
                                                              CIP

Designed by *Rhea Braunstein*

Manufactured in the United States of America

10 9 8 7 6 5 4 3 2 1

First Edition

Acknowledgments

· · · · · ·

The editors wish to thank Toni Sciarra of Prentice Hall Press for the knowledge and assistance she offered in preparing and editing this series. We also wish to acknowledge the many contributions of Dr. Lawrence Balter, our preface writer, and our advisory panel, whose names and affiliations are listed on pages vii–ix; and the writers of this volume, Mary Lee Grisanti, Dian G. Smith, and Dr. Charles Flatter; and researcher Judith Rovenger.

Advisory Panel

• • • • • •

LOUISE BATES AMES, Ph.D., received her degree in psychology from Yale University in 1933 and was a member of the staff of the Yale Clinic of Child Development from 1936 to 1950. In 1950, with colleagues, she founded the Gesell Institute of Human Development. She has written many books on child behavior for parents, including *Is Your Child in the Wrong Grade?*, *Questions Parents Ask: Straight Answers from Louise Bates Ames*, and *What Am I Doing in This Grade: A Book for Parents about School Readiness*.

LAWRENCE BALTER, Ph.D., our preface writer, is Professor of Educational Psychology at New York University, where he is also Director of the Warm Line, a telephone counseling service for parents. Dr. Balter served as President of the Media Psychology Division of the American Psychological Association and has advised thousands of parents through his radio and television programs. Dr. Balter's column, "Routines," appears regularly in *Sesame Street Magazine Parents' Guide*, where he is a contributing editor. He has authored several books for parents, including *Dr. Balter's Child Sense* and *Who's in Control?* as well as *Stepping Stone Stories*—a series of illustrated books to help children cope with problems and fears. Dr. Balter is in private practice in Manhattan.

STELLA CHESS, Ph.D., is Professor of Child Psychiatry at New York University Medical Center where, through the "New York Longitudinal Study," she is involved in ongoing research exploring the importance of temperament. She and her husband, Dr. Alexander Thomas, have coauthored several books, including their most recent work, *Know Your Child*.

E. GERALD DABBS, M.D., is a board-certified child and adolescent psychiatrist in Manhattan. He is also Associate Clinical Professor of Psychiatry at Cornell University Medical College, Director of clinical services at Louise Wise Services, and a private practitioner. Dr. Dabbs has been extensively involved in child-abuse prevention and treatment and works regularly with disadvantaged and adoptive families.

ALICE STERLING HONIG, Ph.D., is Professor of Child Development at Syracuse University and a well-known consultant for child-care and parenting projects. She is the author of *Playtime Learning Games for Young Children*, as well as other books about babies and young children for child-care workers and parents.

JEROME KAGAN, Ph.D., is the Daniel and Amy Starch Professor of Psychology at Harvard University. His research is concerned with the development of children, especially temperamental differences involving qualities of shyness and sociability. His publications include the books *The Nature of the Child* and *The Second Year: The Emergence of Self-Awareness*.

HANNAH NUBA, M.S., is Director of The New York Public Library Early Childhood Resource and Information Center. She holds a master's degree from Columbia University as well as a certification in education and library science from the State University of New York. Her publications include *Resources for Early Childhood* and *Infants: Research and Resources*.

ISTAR SCHWAGER, Ph.D., is Director of Research for the Children's Television Workshop's Magazine Group—including the *Sesame Street Magazine Parents' Guide*. She has worked on the development of television shows, books, toys, and other products. She holds a doctorate in educational psychology and a master's degree in early childhood education. Dr. Schwager has taught at levels from preschool to graduate school and writes frequently for parents.

About the Writers

• • • • • •

MARY LEE GRISANTI has published articles and books on many subjects ranging from espionage to health, and teaches writing at the School of Visual Arts in New York City. She is also the author of a novel, *Rare Earth* (Doubleday). She lives in Connecticut with her husband and daughter.

DIAN G. SMITH is a freelance writer with a master's degree in education from Harvard University. She has written many articles about families and children for national magazines and is the author of four books for young adults and two books for younger children. Her most recent works include *Great American Film Directors* (Julian Messner), *My New Baby and Me* (Metropolitan Museum of Art/Scribners), and *Happy Birthday to Me* (Metropolitan Museum of Art/Scribners). Dian Smith is the mother of three children.

CHARLES H. FLATTER, Ph.D., is Professor of Human Development at the University of Maryland. Dr. Flatter has authored numerous publications, including *Children: Their Growth and Development* (McGraw-Hill), *Help Me*

Learn (Prentice Hall Press), and *Half a Childhood: Time for School-Age Child Care* (School-Age Notes). Dr. Flatter has worked in the area of curriculum development for educational television and serves on the board of advisers for *Sesame Street Magazine Parents' Guide*. He has three children.

Series Introduction

• • • • • •

What do children need to learn about themselves and the world around them if they are to realize their potential? What can parents do to facilitate their children's emotional, physical, and intellectual growth?

For more than a generation, Children's Television Workshop (CTW), creators of *Sesame Street,* has asked these questions and has conducted extensive research to uncover the answers. We have gathered together some of the best minds in child development, health, and communication. We have studied what experts around the world are doing to nurture this generation. And, most important, we have worked with children and parents to get direct feedback on what it means to be a productive and fulfilled family member in our rapidly changing world. We recognize that there are no simple solutions to the inherent complexities of child rearing and that in most situations, there are no single answers that apply to all families. Thus we do not offer a ''how-to'' approach to being a parent. Rather, we present facts where information will help each of you make appropriate decisions, and we offer strategies for finding solutions to the varied concerns of individual families.

The development of the CTW Family Living Series is a natural outgrowth of our commitment to share what we have learned with parents and others who care for today's children. It is hoped that the information presented here will make the job of parenting a little easier—and more fun.

Contents

• • • • • •

CONTENTS

Preface

· · · · · ·

Discipline. There's that word again. To be sure, discipline is one of the most perplexing subjects parents come up against. It is also one of critical importance. After all, the methods we use can have a profound effect on our children's personal development and outlook on life. Our discipline strategies also play a major role in the kind of parent-child relationship that evolves. The road to successful discipline is a winding one with many potential obstacles.

Most of us enter the arena of child rearing with some preconceived notions about discipline. Much of what we know about discipline is the result of what was done to us as children. Sometimes this is good, but more often than not it has drawbacks because it is not tailor-made to fit our unique, present-day situations. Moreover, because we are only human, we parents are subject to personal whims, needs to control, mood swings, frustrations, and a host of other pressures that influence the ways in which we try to manage our children. Clearly, how we react to our kids is not always for their benefit.

One difficulty we have is with the word, discipline, itself. All too frequently, we narrow its meaning so that it becomes synonymous with punishment. This creates more problems than it solves primarily because it limits our options. We can become locked into tit-for-tat contests with our children, and this can cause damage to their self-esteem. Once we begin to rely on retaliation, admonition, retribution, and other forms of inflicting penalties, we are on a downward spiral. The most disturbing end result of this descent is, of course, when humiliation and physical punishment are introduced.

In punishment-based discipline, discipline becomes a situational issue, when, in fact, true discipline is interwoven into the fabric of our everyday lives with our kids. It concerns our way of speaking to one another. It has to do with the decision to help, or refrain from helping, a child with a school project that has been put off until the last minute of the night before it is due. Discipline comes into play when you must decide whether to insist that your daughter practice the piano before her next lesson. It is how you react when your son simply forgets to put his soiled clothes into the hamper or refuses to feed the dog. It permeates every interaction we have with our children, and it works best when thought of in a very positive light: protecting and guiding our children toward greater self-control and good judgment, rather than simply demanding their obedience.

In this book, the common, daily struggles parents and children confront, and each must somehow endure, such as bedtime and bathtime, are placed in a useful perspective. We are treated to seeing these bits of daily activity in the context of something larger, namely, the importance of routine in a child's life. Children require a measure of regularity and predictability in their lives for a sense of security to evolve. Clearly, discipline seen in this light will help reduce the arbitrariness that so often leads to useless hassles between parent and child.

Disciplining requires an understanding of child development. Normal children are curious, impatient, and active.

They want to try new things. They want to know how things work—no matter that it may be dangerous or off-limits for them. Both toddlers and teens oppose you in order to distinguish themselves from you. For each of them, it is an identity issue. Preschoolers act bossy and flout your authority as they wrestle with mastering the world around them. Knowing what motivates children is invaluable in planning ways to peacefully coexist. Properly forewarned, we can prepare ourselves with strategies that will enable us to curtail potential skirmishes. *Parents' Guide to Understanding Discipline* provides a subtext that reminds us that children are constantly changing and that we, as parents, must keep abreast of these shifts and continually realign ourselves to their emerging needs.

I am going to conclude with a very trite statement, namely, that love, trust, and encouragement are the principal ingredients for authentic and dependable disciplining. By offering information about child development, the role that temperament plays in children's behavior, and loads of practical suggestions for dealing with situations that parents find exasperating, I believe that this book will prove to be an indispensable guide to the strategies you need for effective discipline.

LAWRENCE BALTER, PH.D.

A Few Words About Pronouns

• • • • • •

The child fell off *his* bike." Or how about "The child fell off *her* bike"? Then again we could say, "The child fell off *his or her* bike." How to deal with pronouns?

If you are a regular reader of *Sesame Street Magazine Parents' Guide,* you know that our policy is to alternate the use of gender-related pronouns. In one paragraph we say *his;* in the following one we use *her.* In a book, that specific policy is not quite as practical—there are just too many paragraphs—but it works in a general way by alternating chapters.

Introduction

• • • • • •

If parents were asked to choose one word to sum up what they feel toward their children, that single word would overwhelmingly be *love.* The love we have for our children is deep and forgiving. Sometimes it takes us by surprise—it is simply so strong.

Discipline is the other word in child rearing, the one that comes to mind when loving doesn't seem to be enough. It's the word that comes after "but"—as in, "I love my child, but . . ." We tend not to think about discipline until we find that we are frustrated, angry, or otherwise uncomfortable with a child.

Yet discipline is more than the art and science of saying no to children. More than any other word, it encompasses the wide range of beliefs and practices we rely on to raise children. Discipline is not just about getting children to go to bed peacefully at night, to forgo expensive toys seen on television, to do their homework, or to come home at curfew time; it is about helping children to grow into nice, healthy, independent human beings: people who respect themselves and others.

The goals of discipline and the goals of love are, in the end, the same. A child's ability to care about getting enough sleep, to be cooperative and to be honest—in other words, to care about himself—comes from the way he is cared for. And only a person who cares about himself can care about other people.

We are concerned about "effective" discipline—finding strategies that work. But in essence, what we really want to know is, How can I say no to my child's behavior and still say yes to my child? How can I get him to share my concern for him?

Self-care, self-control, and socially appropriate and sensitive behaviors all begin with a child's secure sense of himself, of his own worth as a separate and unique human being. Children who are treated with respect are more likely to learn self-respect, which is the basis of respecting the rights of others. This is why a book about discipline must start as a book about love, because love is the context in which discipline is understood. Love is the warm climate in which children can change and grow.

PART I

······

Laying the Foundation

"Well I didn't have the advantage of obedience school, you know."

CHAPTER ONE

······

Learning Love and Respect

We begin to communicate our tenderness toward our children in the way we first hold them and feed them, bathe and clothe them, talk to them, and play with them. As they move from babyhood to childhood, our love for them remains constant but our communication with them often falters. What happens when a toddler repeatedly wants to pull the safety plugs out of an electrical outlet, an eight year old refuses to do her homework, or a preadolescent begins to experiment with alcohol? We find many ways to say no. After all, we're trying to protect her. Lost in the translation is the phrase ''because I love you.'' How do we discipline effectively yet in a way that lets the child still *feel* loved—even when she is driving us crazy?

It is one thing to love a child; it is another thing entirely for a child to feel loved. Underlying all *constructive* discipline is the steady message: What you are doing is not okay with me, but you yourself *are* okay, and you always will be. This is basic respect for the child as a human being with a right to exist, to be loved, and to sometimes be in trouble. It seems simple, but like all simple truths it can slip out of focus in the day-to-day struggles of being a parent.

Alice Miller, a noted psychoanalyst and the author of a number of highly acclaimed books about childhood, writes in *For Your Own Good:* ''Children need emotional and physical support from the adult. This must include the following

3

elements: (1) Respect for the child, (2) Respect for his needs, (3) Tolerance for his feelings, and (4) Willingness to learn from his behavior.''

Miller does not use the word *love*, but this is a very good description of love in action.

Like many contemporary studies, Alice Miller's book raises serious questions about the theories of child rearing that were prevalent in the West well into the 1950s. Like Miller, many of today's child-care experts recognize that children who were treated as part of an authoritarian hierarchy in which the father, like the king, was the boss of the family, the mother was next in line in authority, and the children owed obedience to both of them were often denied the respect they needed to thrive. The 1960s heralded a change that still affects us today: The individual became the focus. No longer was the child reared to fit in, but rather she was encouraged to stand out, to pursue her own goals, and concentrate on her own fulfillment. Like all change, the move from totalitarian parenting to extremely empathetic parenting wrought some good and some bad. On the good side, the rights of a child to be nurtured rather than simply molded were taken seriously. On the bad side, a child's right to the security of limits was overlooked.

Overlooked, too, were the rights of parents. Perhaps most sadly, the permissive approach (or nonapproach) to discipline that became popular in the '60s produced some very lost children whose needs were disregarded as surely as they had been by totalitarian parents. Sometimes parents' laissez-faire attitudes were merely a mask for disinterest and convenience on the part of parents whose minds were on their *own* pursuits. But often, too, parents had begun to wonder themselves just what was right and wrong. This confusion could not help but engender anger on both parents' and children's parts. Parents were angry because they had given up control to children who were unable to handle it, and children acted out their own insecurity. No one was in charge.

The end result of both permissive and totalitarian parenting is a tacit rejection of the child. Whether the child is squeezed into a conformity or left to wander on an open prairie of too many choices and not enough caring, the message is the same: *You* are not important.

The limits we set for our children become, in time, the limits that they set for themselves. If we push too hard, we risk raising a child who is unable to make conscientious decisions, who is fearful, and who is more concerned with the rules than with right or wrong. If, on the other hand, we do not push back when our children push *us*, then we risk raising children without a sense of boundaries and without a sense of self.

To relinquish parental responsibility by not disciplining our children is akin to deliberately letting go of a child's hand in a crowd. To relinquish that responsibility by disciplining too severely, however, is like holding on to a child's hand until she becomes an adult—at which point she will lack the experience she needs to handle herself securely.

How can parents instill the security of boundaries without suppressing their child's natural exuberance? Dorothy Corkille Briggs, a parent educator and author of *Your Child's Self-Esteem*, lists six types of safety children need to experience as they grow into responsive and responsible adults.

The safety of trust. Trust means that our children know we are there and that we can be counted on to continue to be there. Children can trust us when they know that we mean what we say and do what we say we'll do. Trust requires honesty; we cannot teach trust if we make threats that cannot be carried out, or that, if carried out, are too severe to be fair. We cannot teach trust if we make promises that we intend to break. Trust also requires that we treat the child as a person who has a right to know what we think and feel and yet still protect her right to be a child by shielding her from things that are inappropriate.

For example, eight-year-old John comes home from his baseball game and finds that his mother is visibly tense. John asks her what is wrong. If she says, ''Nothing,'' John will begin to think of anything and everything that *he* may have done to cause his mother's anxiety. This is a natural reaction. Children live in self-centered worlds; they assume that everything has to do with them. John will probably conclude that he has done something wrong, or worse, that something about *him* is wrong.

If John's mother says, ''Sorry, I'm waiting for an important phone call that has nothing to do with you.'' John will be curious and possibly concerned, but he will not feel personally threatened. He can express his concern by asking her to tell him more. She may say she doesn't want to talk right now—that's fair enough. Perhaps, one day if John wants to be alone, she'll remember to respect his privacy, too.

Or she may tell him what's on her mind. If she's worried about her job or something similar, she can tell him in words he'll understand. If it's about something more frightening, for example, sickness or marital problems, she must be extra-careful to tell John only as much as he seems to need to hear now and in a way that makes it clear that it has nothing to do with him. Regardless of how much she chooses to share, her directness lays the foundation for John's trust in her.

Trust means inviting your child's confidence in you; this will become her confidence in herself.

Honesty, however, is not the only thing that inspires trust. *How* we express our feelings toward our children is as important as the information we deliver. And that brings us to the safety of nonjudgment.

Nonjudgment. The old saying "Sticks and stones may break my bones, but words can never hurt me" is not entirely true. Words *can* hurt. When unkind words are repeated over and over, they can cause lasting damage.

Most of us would cringe at deliberately calling a child stupid or ugly, or any other nasty name. But what we say in a moment of intense anger quite often blames or labels a child in a most destructive way.

To be nonjudgmental is to separate the child's behavior from the child. It requires first that when we are angry we make an effort to stop for a second and sort out our feelings (this is a terrific idea in and of itself).

One method for fostering nonjudgmental interactions with our children is getting into the habit of making "I-statements" instead of "You-statements." For example, instead of saying, "You're such a pig!" or "How can you live in such a dump?" you can say, "I need to have order in the house; so many things all over the place make me nervous." By making I-statements we articulate accurately how the behavior makes us feel and we focus on the consequence—for us—of the behavior, not on the behavior itself. No one gets blamed.

This takes practice, but is very rewarding for both the child and ourselves. Somehow honestly and emphatically endorsing our own feelings almost always makes us feel better. Children are free to respond to the problem that their behavior causes and are less likely to dig in and react defensively because they haven't been attacked.

Cherishing. It may seem odd to make a special point of saying that children must be cherished. We cherish our children by virtue of the fact that they are ours. It goes without saying.

Unfortunately, cherishing is all too often left unexpressed. We love our children, but we usually only remember that we love them when we think about losing them or when they have done something we are proud of. We notice them when they win our attention with good performance or when they command our attention by misbehaving. We forget to take the time just to notice them being their lovable little selves. This is not a matter of "catch your child being good," but of "catch your child being herself" and show her that you like it.

All people, but especially children, want and need to be loved for who they *are* simply because they're there, unique and unrepeatable. This means paying attention, listening deeply, and noticing the tiny things that make each child an individual: a dimple, a throaty chuckle, a special look. It means that when we are with the child we are really *there*, not mentally writing a list of what needs to be bought on the weekend or what needs to be finished at the office.

Children are even more adept than adults at perceiving when a person they're with is really elsewhere. We've all had this experience: If a waiter brings our order well-done when we'd ordered it rare, we're merely annoyed, but if our mate barely looks up from the paper as we discuss our day, we're more likely to feel hurt. Children who sense they have been left "alone" by an adult whose mind is elsewhere feel more than hurt; they feel afraid. They depend for survival on the loving attentiveness of their parents. This is true for adolescents as much as it is for infants.

Owning feelings. As a natural extension of feeling cherished for the good person she is, a child needs to know that even her negative feelings are okay. Allowing your child to own her own feelings means remembering to acknowledge that she is a good person even if not all of her feelings or behaviors are so endearing. For example, when a fight erupts over the dump trucks in the sandbox, three-year-old Tanya punches her playmate, Mike. Tanya's mother says, "Tanya! You don't want to punch Mike—he's your best friend!" Tanya's mother has just asked her daughter to ignore her own feelings—anger—and feel what Mom prefers Tanya to feel: friendliness. The message is that Tanya's feelings are wrong and bad. When this happens often enough, children conclude that because they so often feel the "wrong" thing, there must be something wrong with them.

Allowing your child to own her feelings, however, does not mean letting her do whatever she wants. Tanya's mother could say, "You're really mad at Mike, but you cannot hit him. Why don't you play with your truck on the grass for a while, until you're ready to play with Mike again?"

This is a quite trivial example, but the occasions on which we subtly preempt children's feelings are frequent and mundane: "You don't want to eat all that ice cream, dinner is almost ready," "You're too old to be afraid of the dark," "You should enjoy the museum," and "You don't really want to hurt the baby."

Letting a child own her feelings reassures a child that

even when she feels differently from you, you will not withdraw your love. Telling a child she ought to feel differently than she does implies that she is okay only when she feels the way she "should" feel.

As children get older and more able to put their feelings into words, encouraging them to talk about their feelings often helps them open up about the things that bother them the most.

Empathy. Empathy is a corollary of allowing children to own their own feelings. It requires you to acknowledge how the child feels *and to try to see it from her point of view.*

Jenny, for example, is horrified at the earthworm she finds in the garden. Her mother is tempted to say, "But honey, worms are good for the garden; they let air into the soil." This is true and enlightens Jenny, but it does not acknowledge her legitimate right to have a negative reaction to something new and slimy. Instead, Jenny's mother says, "Well, that is really pretty yucky, isn't it? But, you know, it is lucky that we have some worms in the garden . . ." Now she is showing empathy for her daughter's feelings—which makes it much easier for the little girl to listen to the explanation her mother provides. She can understand more easily now because she feels understood.

Empathy, though, is also more subtle. Children feel things very intensely. Because there are many things outside their control in their lives, this means they often feel intense negative feelings such as anger, frustration, fear, and disappointment. These strong negative emotions cause them—and us—stress. Yet we are often tempted to withdraw our support when they need it most by explaining away their stresses or even denying them.

Empathy requires many of the same "noticing skills" as cherishing. For instance, children who are upset about one thing are likely to talk about something else or to act out the problem rather than deal with it directly. It's up to parents to pick up the signals. Nine-year-old Jeff, for example, just wouldn't do his homework, but he insisted that nothing was wrong at school. He did, however, talk a lot about two other boys in his class—boys known to be cutups. It turned out that he felt hurt and rejected because the teacher had picked *them* to be in the school play but not him. By not doing his homework he was "getting back" at the teacher. He was also forcing his parents to take notice of him—something he really needed then.

Being watchful of a child's body language is also vital. A child who's overly rambunctious or who won't look you in the eye may be communicating a need for attention rather than merely being contrary. Making the effort to read your child's signals sends a powerful message that you care and understand.

Unique growing. As children mature they go through many predictable stages. Two year olds are notorious for saying no and nine year olds, in general, would not be caught dead playing with a member of the opposite sex. But within these general guidelines, every child grows in her own unique way.

Growth is not a straightforward, linear process. There is an old Russian proverb that says, in effect, that to live a life is not as simple as to cut across a field. Children jump, lurch, dawdle, and meander as they grow. Sometimes they jump, lurch, dawdle, or meander backward and sideways as well as forward. Sometimes they wander onto dangerous ground; sometimes they merely get lost. We must be there to guide them and to gently nudge them toward maturity. We can neither push them nor hold them back. Our response to them must change and grow as they do.

When four-year-old Danielle's mother nursed their new baby, Danielle suddenly told her mother she wanted to nurse, too. If her mother had replied that nursing was just for babies, Danielle would have been embarrassed by her desire; she would have been made to feel like a baby. If her mother had allowed her to suck, she would have missed an opportunity to help Danielle along on her road to maturity. Rather, Danielle's mom chose to cuddle her little girl in her arms while telling her the loving story of how she used to nurse Danielle, too. She ended the story by reminding Danielle just how much she had grown up and how proud her mom was of her. By not challenging her, Mom let Danielle reassure herself that indeed she was not a baby any more.

Letting our children know that they are growing and that they can continue to grow at their own rate lets them know that we have confidence that they are growing just fine. Growing up means change and uncertainty. If our children know that we have faith in them, they can deal with the changes in their own way, knowing that it's okay to be themselves.

When children know they are believed in, listened to, understood, cared for, and respected—in other words, when children feel they are loved—they are open to the principles of effective discipline. As we discipline effectively, we help our children to grow in maturity and understanding.

Effective discipline'' is based on the following ideas.

- We want to discipline children in ways that are appropriate to their age and development. Just as a two year old cannot learn to ride a two-wheel bicycle, neither can she negotiate other tasks that are not congruent with her individual growth pattern, for example, sharing favorite toys. Likewise, a preteen cannot be expected to handle the demands of peer pressure alone. She needs her parents' guidance.

  In tailoring discipline to a child's age and stage of development, there is no substitute for knowing your own unique child and knowing yourself well enough to match *your* expectations to her abilities. This is the key not only to solving problems, but to preventing them.
- We also want to discipline in constructive, character-building ways, rather than in critical, ego-destroying ways. This means showing respect for a child's accomplishments *and* mistakes. Someone who is imperfect gets better and better. Someone who is expected to be perfect can only fail every day.
- We want to discipline fairly so that children learn to share our values, rather than just to obey in order to avoid punishment. Inherent in fairness is a willingness to put ourselves on the line: to behave according to the same standards we have for our children and to be honest about it when we fall short of these standards.
- We want to communicate well so that our children understand our desires and demands and so that they, too, can learn to communicate well and don't have to act out their frustrations.

Ultimately, effective discipline involves being consistent in responding to the unique needs of each child in the family. It also involves a willingness to look beyond our own upbringing as a model for parenthood. We want to decide what kind of discipline we are comfortable with, and not automatically act as our parents did. We want to be able to like our children as well as love them. And we want them to like themselves.

CHAPTER TWO

......

What Can We Reasonably Expect from Our Children?

It's an old joke that we don't get to choose our parents; but the joke is on parents, too, because we don't get to choose our kids, either. You may have reflected on this, once or twice, when you were watching your toddler strew spaghetti across a restaurant table or when your eighth grader, who willingly went to school this morning looking like an All-American kid, announced this afternoon that he wants to have his ear pierced as his friends have done.

And if it isn't enough that our children surprise us with sudden demands for independence, sometimes it even seems as if our children cannot be ours at all! Their personalities are so at odds with ours, we wonder whether the hospital could have given us the wrong kids.

Of course, some children *do* seem to be born into the "right" families. A bubbly, vivacious mother has a gregarious little boy who steps right up and shakes hands; a father who's a historian has a daughter who loves to read and who loves to write in her journal. These parents can easily recognize themselves in their kids, can understand what motivates them, and can easily find a common ground with them.

But what happens when an even-tempered, laid-back mom gives birth to a high-energy, hot-tempered daughter?

Or when a sports-minded, outgoing dad sires a reflective, musically inclined son? These parents will have to work a little harder to find a common ground with their kids. If they don't, they may find themselves constantly locked in conflict with their children, asking them to conform in ways that are nearly impossible. What accounts for these differences in personality? How can a parent work with, rather than against, a child who is very different from himself?

Nurturing According to Nature

Before we became parents, it was relatively easy to decide what child-rearing issues were important to us and how we would choose to discipline our children. Faced with a real live child who does not fit into our preconceived notion of what a child should be, however, we can feel frustrated, even lost.

The "nature vs. nurture" argument regarding child development has been around a long time. Simply put, the "nature" side argues that most, if not all, of a person's personality traits are inborn, while the "nurture" proponents maintain that what is learned through experience shapes personality.

In modern times, one slant on the nature philosophy has been psychoanalytic theory, which evolved from the work of Sigmund Freud. According to Freud's theories, which have been modified and adapted by many of his successors, all children's behavior is motivated by "instinctual drives." In other words, children are more or less primitive little human animals driven to fulfill their self-centered desires for food, comfort, and pleasure until those urges are brought under control by his parents and society. Psychoanalytic ideas about the repression and denial of feelings still seem to hold a certain amount of truth, but not the whole truth.

An older version of the nature philosophy, but one that has recently been renewed, holds that children *inherit* all of their characteristics—their talents, their temperaments, their intelligence—in much the same way that they inherit their eye color or blood type. In other words, we are born more or less the persons we will always be and there's not much we can do about changing what we start out with.

Current research in child development shows that many of a person's attributes *are* more or less present at birth, for example, a tendency toward shyness, or reticence. Yet, we have also learned that the conditions in which a child grows from infancy to adulthood may directly influence later behavior. Those who favor the nurture philosophy believe that changing the experiences of a child *can* change his actions, his temperament, and even his intelligence. This philosophy is reflected in the thinking of behavioral psychologists whose work is based on the theories of Ivan Pavlov, a Russian scientist. Pavlov demonstrated that what we call learning is, to our nervous systems, a matter of conditioned reflexes. By changing the types of conditioning, behaviorists say, profound changes in behavior and personality will result.

The problem with these philosophies is that as much as they explain, there is much that they *don't* account for. The richness and variety of human experience—and the common sense we acquire as parents—teach us that we have not yet found a theory that completely describes how all children grow. Those who love children and work closely with them have probably always sensed intuitively that children grow best when they are nurtured in a way that is attuned to their individual natures. Each child's nature invites, even demands, a certain type of nurturing, and children blossom when their care givers are able to respond to these needs.

Today we know that infants are indeed born into this world with very distinct natures that make each one different from the other. Babies are as much persons as adults are, and they are very much themselves right from the start. Once we acknowledge that our children have unique personalities just as we do, it is easier to realize that we cannot speak only of the influence that parents exert on children; we must acknowledge that *we* are influenced by our children, too. A baby who is irritable and cries more than a contented baby trains his parents to respond to him in a different way. And parents, in turn, react according to their own temperaments. One kind of parent may become very responsive to his needs; another might learn to tune him out.

As such a child becomes more verbal and more independent, his loud and intense way of dealing with the world will elicit very different responses from everyone in his orbit; his parents, teachers, and age-mates, in turn, will bring their own personality traits into play when they respond to him. His parents will probably find that he responds best to a different sort of discipline, too. One discipline style, for instance, may involve getting him away from the agitation of other children momentarily and limiting the stimuli to which he is exposed. When he is a preschooler, sensitive parents may take care to provide a little down time at a birthday party so he doesn't get too revved up. When he is a grade schooler, they may keep overnights with friends to a minimum, for example.

Your Own Unique Child

Drs. Stella Chess and Alexander Thomas conducted one of the longest and most important studies of childhood development, the "New York Longitudinal Study," at New York Hospital. Beginning in the 1950s, they followed a large number of children over 30 years, from infancy into adulthood. They observed infants and their parents, watched them interact, and then recorded how the children grew by interviewing them at certain intervals.

Chess and Thomas noted that parents who could correctly pick up their children's individual signals and respond appropriately had much more harmonious and enjoyable relationships with their children than did parents who could not get in tune with their children. The children of parents who responded appropriately to their particular needs and personalities grew up happier and more confident.

Chess and Thomas also found that temperamental traits seem to fall into nine general categories, which they describe in their book *Know Your Child*.

1. **Activity Level.** The highly active infant is the one who is always terrifying his parents by trying to roll off the bed or changing table. He is almost always in motion. Highly active *does not* signify the disorder known as hyperactivity, which must be diagnosed by a pediatric neurologist and which is characterized by an accompanying attention-span problem.

   A low-activity baby is generally placid and slow moving. He is much easier to watch as a toddler, but he can be irritating in his pokiness as he grows up. Although many children can be described either as highly active or low-activity types, the majority fall somewhere in between.

2. **Rhythmicity or Regularity.** A very regular baby is one who usually sleeps, eats, and has bowel movements at the same hour every day. Obviously, this makes his parents' life easier. Such a child may be relatively easy to toilet train.

A child who is irregular gets tired or hungry at different times every day. He is typically the center of mealtime conflicts because he is not hungry during the family dinner hour but may be hungry sometime before or after. The irregular child needs a wholly different approach to toilet training—one that makes him more aware of his body so that he can alert his parents, because his parents won't be able to guess in advance.

3. **Approach or Withdrawal.** An infant who laps up a new food the first time it's offered, who splashes like a whale in his tub the minute he hits the water, or who smiles immediately and reaches out for new people has quick positive responses. This can make life for his family a lot easier, because he will initially cope well with changes such as starting school. This easy approach can also make him impulsive, so his parents will have to teach him a degree of caution to rein in his exuberance.

Withdrawal is shown by infants who reject their first foods and who turn away in fright or displeasure the first time a new toy is dangled in front of them. Such a child needs more patience and understanding; he needs to get used to things slowly.

4. **Adaptability.** The highly adaptable child can adjust to new situations easily. He takes to routines and to changes in routines rapidly. However, a highly adaptable child can suddenly get on a new schedule of waking during the night after waking up two nights in a

row teething. Because of his inclination to conform, he can also have a hard time standing up for himself in a group.

Low adaptability means that children take change hard. Their parents must use patience and persistence to get them to accept new routines, and they must be very consistent in their methods of discipline.

5. **Sensory Threshold.** A high sensory threshold will make a child less sensitive to foods and to the sights and sounds around him, helping him to nap through noise and to eat whatever's offered him—even if it's spicy.

Coping with a low sensory threshold, however, can pose many problems. Children with low thresholds often react negatively to loud noises and changes in the texture of their food or clothing. With this kind of temperamental trait, a birthday party can be overwhelming, and adjusting to mild alterations in taste or smell, such as eating a new brand of tuna fish or wearing clothes washed in a new detergent, may prove very distressing.

6&7. **Quality of Mood** & **Intensity of Expressiveness.** These two qualities are quite often seen together. Children with a negative quality of mood and low intensity of expressiveness often fail to react to a situation the way their parents believe they should. For instance, they may not give any sign that they enjoy special treats, and will respond to everything in a very low-key way. Obviously, they may provoke a less enthusiastic response from their parents than do children who are openly expressive and show delight when something special comes their way.

Yet very intense children are often loud and difficult. Their responses to frustration are off the Richter scale, and they can be the scourge of birthday parties. Because we are so conscious of mood and intensity in social interactions, overly loud or too low-key children can turn people off—including their parents. They need special understanding.

8. **Distractibility.** A highly distractible toddler is easier to manage than one with low distractibility because toddler management consists almost exclusively of constantly redirecting the child's attention away from inappropriate things and on to appropriate ones. But the opposite is true once the child gets to school, where the inability to sit still and stick to one subject at a time is a liability. Parents often mistake high distractibility for disobedience because highly distractible children often leave one task unfinished as they move to the next.

Children with low distractibility can become very responsible; they have the intense concentration necessary to complete involved projects. But they can also miss out on things going on around them because their attention is so closely focused.

9. **Persistence and Attention Span.** High distractibility is similar to low attention span, but a distractible child with high persistence is able to turn away from his distractions and stick with a task. Unfortunately these traits are usually found in the opposite combination. Because we put a high value on persistence—in our schools, in our families, and in our society as a whole—low attention span tends to become connected to low self-esteem. Highly persistent youngsters can sometimes run into trouble, too. They find it very hard to be flexible; if rules are changed, they resent it and cannot "go with the flow."

Chess and Thomas suggest that in most normal children these temperamental qualities are combined into one of three patterns, which they call the "easy" child, the "difficult" child, and the "slow-to-warm-up" child. They believe that when parents speak of an "easy" or a "difficult" child, they are often, in fact, referring to inborn temperamental attributes. This is obviously of the greatest importance in knowing how to deal with problems; if a child won't wear what you pick out because he has a low sensory threshold and wool irritates his skin—something a three year old might have real difficulty putting into words—that is quite different from the defiant displays of independence children of that age tend to make. If a child has trouble in school because he finds it hard to break off one activity and move to the next—the attribute of persistence—the teacher needs to know that this child requires a different response from one who is simply testing the limits.

Recently, and with good reason, the notion of the difficult child (chapter 10) has received wide attention. When we understand that what makes a child "difficult" may be temperamental attributes over which he has no control, we may find it much easier to overcome our frustrations and achieve a good fit with such a child.

On the other hand, temperamentally easy children may be so compliant that parents become inadvertently desensitized to their legitimate wants and needs. Such children can later have problems resisting peer pressure and forming an independent identity.

The "slow-to-warm-up" child is the one who tends to hang back right from the start. His initial reaction to new people and new situations is to withdraw. Naturally, such children don't usually get the warm, accepting response that more outgoing children garner. Yet with sensitivity and guidance, these children can overcome their instinctual reactions and learn to relate to the world in a way that brings them more positive feedback.

It is important to remember that temperament is a normal part of every personality. Every child has some of these attributes to one degree or another—and so does every parent. One parent may delight in a child whose voracious interest in nature extends as far as having lizards for pets; another parent might relate better to a kid who prefers to merely *read* about reptiles. Parents also have a right to express themselves and to have their needs met. The sports-minded father should not be expected to give up every softball game to attend recitals with his musically inclined son. Some kind of compromise and accommodation of *each* person's needs must be sought.

Parents are entitled to have and to set expectations for their children, for without expectations children won't know what to do. But these expectations must be realistic. Insisting that a reticent eighth-grade girl try out for cheerleading would be cruel, but seeing to it that she has a number of rewarding group activities in her schedule—perhaps Girl Scouts or swimming—supports her and gives her the opportunity to enjoy experiences that she might not take the initiative to seek on her own.

How the Environment Helps or Hinders Growth

Each one of us has an inborn set of qualities that can be described as temperament, as well as certain intellectual and physical capacities. Yet, how these qualities and capacities are developed depends almost wholly on how we are treated.

Recently psychologists have become interested in what

they call the "resilient" child: The child who, despite being exposed to many stresses and disadvantages, still grows up to be a happy and productive person. Emmy E. Werner, Ph.D., is one of the authors of a 30-year longitudinal study on the Hawaiian island of Kauai that set out to study the long-term results of biological and psychological stresses on children (the effects of problems that occurred while the baby was still in the womb or at the time of birth and emotional problems in the family such as divorce and alcoholism).

Surprisingly, the Kauai study found that by the age of 10, some "high-risk" children who had been subject to such stresses were doing just as well as children who had no birth problems and who came from untroubled homes. Dr. Werner and the other researchers began to look for what they called the "protective factors" in these children's lives.

Some of the protective factors came from the children themselves: In general, they were temperamentally active, outgoing, and relaxed. Some of the protective factors came from the environment: Oldest girls and firstborn sons in families where children were spaced at least two years apart seemed to fare better, too.

But most importantly, these children had experienced steady love and guidance from at least one person during their early years. These were children who had learned that there was someone they could count on (often a grandparent)—both for love and for limits. Dr. Werner points out that structure and rules in the household as well as assigned chores were part of the daily routine for these children (especially boys) during childhood and adolescence.

The Kauai study shows that parents can actively shape an environment in which their child will prosper. It solidly supports the idea that with the right kind of nurturing children can surmount even the most serious stresses.

But what is the right kind of nurturing? Just as nature and nurture are balanced in a changing dynamic, parents and children are involved in an unceasing dynamic of predicting and provoking each other's behavior. And as children develop, the dynamic continues to change. Because each child, and each parent, is an individual, and because their relationship must constantly grow and change, it is not possible to say that there is any right way to raise all children or any methods of discipline that will work with all children in the same situation. The important thing, most experts agree, is what is called "a good fit" between individual parents and an individual child.

Finding a Good Fit

How can we ensure a good fit, especially when our children's personalities seem to be at odds with ours? A good fit between parent and child can be achieved when parents match their expectations to their child's ability to respond to those expectations. Although we needn't ignore our own needs or disregard our own personalities, we are the ones who must do most of the adjusting.

As far as effective discipline goes, matching our expectations to our children's abilities depends on two things:

- **Understanding what is appropriate to the child's age and stage of development.** All normal children share certain predictable sequences of growth in all domains of development: physical, emotional, social, and intellectual, or cognitive. By recognizing that a two year old is incapable of sharing, that a six year old cannot be held accountable for keeping his room clean without his parents' help, or that an eleven year old *needs* approval from his peers, for instance, we can better determine how discipline issues should be addressed for each child at each stage of development.

This does not mean that a new method for every child must be cooked up every time you need it. Precisely because children do share similar growth patterns, what works with most three year olds who tell lies, for example, will probably work with yours. But the appropriate response to a three year old telling lies is different from that toward a nine year old, because the intellectual and emotional worlds of three year olds and nine year olds are quite different.

- **Understanding what is appropriate to your child as an individual human being.** Every child is a unique human being with a distinct temperament and his own way of learning and growing up. With temperament, as with age, there are predictable qualities that children with different temperaments share. What works for children who are highly distractible—for instance, getting a toddler to give up an undesirable plaything such as a pen for a desirable one such as a doll—will not be the same as what works for a child who has a hard time disconnecting from one activity and engaging in the next.

Goodness of fit does *not* mean giving in to everything the child wants. Children, no matter what their temperament, need limits in order to become decent human beings. Nor does goodness of fit mean having to rework your own personality so that it better matches the personality of your child. In fact, having too similar a nature to your child can cause problems. For instance, a father who is shy and reticent may find it very hard to encourage a shy and reticent child to participate in the kind of social experiences that he needs. A mother who is as intense and quick to anger as her son may find herself locked in a destructive battle of wills. Nonetheless, dissimilar temperaments are more often the cause of conflicts. Outgoing parents can easily lose patience with shy children, and slow-to-anger adults may feel alienated from explosive children.

The important thing is that all parents know their children's, and their own, limitations, and remain flexible enough to adapt within those limitations. A hot-tempered father is just as able as a more tranquil dad to help an intense child learn to control his outbursts by role-playing with him, teaching him to think, and to talk his way through confrontations. (These kinds of communication skills are discussed in detail in chapter 4.)

Goodness of fit also requires a willingness to adapt, and it depends on parents being tuned in to their child. The real payoff for this attention is that parents can avoid discipline problems *before* they get started. Tuned-in parents are less often in the position of demanding a behavior from a child that he is simply not capable of.

Taking the time to create a good fit circumvents frustration and discouragement and is probably the single most productive ''disciplinary measure'' we can take. It also is the most effective for our children, because it protects their self-esteem against the experience of repeated failure to measure up to unreachable standards and the disapproval that follows that failure.

In essence, a good fit within the family allows for differences: It allows for temperament, for different ways of handling problems within each family—even for different definitions of what constitutes a problem. A good fit between parent and child is sort of like a good fit in a sweater: It gives and breathes, it moves when you move, but it's still there keeping you warm.

Age Appropriateness

Given the range of theories of child development, it should come as no surprise that there is only a minimal consensus as to what children may be capable of at each age. There is a significant amount of overlap at different stages. For many developmental milestones, walking, for instance, there are wide windows of time during which normal children may achieve numerous skills. One child may walk at eight months and another at 1⅓ years and both are still normal. The same applies to behavior.

What follows are a few meaningful generalizations about the major stages of child development from infants to preteens. For more information on exactly what your child may be up to at any given age, books by Erik Erikson, Arnold Gesell, and Jean Piaget are basic academic works in this field. T. Berry Brazelton has written extensively for the layman about babies and younger children. Most federal, state, and local mental health associations publish helpful material on child development as well.

Babies

One of the most fascinating things about Chess and Thomas' study (outlined on pages 19–23) and about much of the recent research on infants is how much infants are *people* right from the beginning. Their personalities are evident in their contentment, their activity level, and their curiosity. Within the first few weeks of life, they can imitate facial expressions and communicate vocally and through gestures.

Babies begin to adapt to their surroundings immediately, and if they are treated with sensitivity and consistency the seeds of cooperation and compliance can be planted. Dr. Alice Honig, a noted psychologist and author of many works about discipline, believes there are *no* discipline issues in the first year of life. Babies will rarely "demand" much more attention than they need. As the La Leche League puts it, "What babies want, babies need." Infants are developmentally incapable of manipulating your behavior. Indeed, studies have shown that babies who were picked up as soon as they cried in the first six months of life were much more cooperative in the second six months and were more often able to wait for their mother's attention without crying.

A high degree of dependency is a common and absolutely normal part of development for many babies. By the age of eight months, some children adamantly demand full-time attention and balk if their parents, particularly their mothers, leave the room. One-year-old Becky, for example, wailed whenever her mother picked up her briefcase and headed toward the door. Her mother couldn't help feeling that her daughter waited until just that last crucial minute to demand her attention, so Mom usually tried to sneak out while Becky was playing. This tactic was bound to get Becky even more upset and even more clingy whenever her mother was at home.

Most babies this age have a hard time seeing their mothers leave the house. They understand only what happens in the here and now and not a few hours from now. In other words, they understand that Mother is going away, but they cannot conceptualize her coming back. Furthermore, many psychologists believe that at around the age of one (and often earlier), a child begins to perceive that his mother is not just an extension of himself, but a wholly separate person with the ability to come and go when *she* wants to.

Becky's mother needed to be reassured that her child was not manipulating her by crying every time she went out. Saying ''bye-bye'' and enduring the screams, she found, was the quickest way to change this behavior. Becky was able to learn that Mother does not disappear on a whim and forever but that she goes and comes back when she says she will. Giving infants the security they need is the surest way of avoiding problems as they grow into toddlers and become more independent.

Toddlers

Like infants', toddlers' behavior is largely based on fulfilling their own needs. Toddlers' needs are to move and explore and to assert themselves as independent persons while still basking in the safety of their parents' constant attention.

The best way to avoid discipline problems with a toddler is to create an environment that the toddler can explore without hurting himself or driving you crazy. Child proofing your home means not only removing obstacles from your child's path and protecting him from electric shocks and other things that can harm him, it also means setting up an environment in which he is free to be curious, to touch and feel and taste and experience things without having to be constantly told no. In a toddler-friendly environment, he is free to discover and master his world, and his parents are free from worrying about him destroying *their* world.

Throughout childhood, behavior is critically affected by basic physical needs, such as the need to sleep and the need to eat. Sometimes it's hard to see that your toddler is being ornery or frenzied merely because he's tired. He can't tell you that that is what's bothering him, and it would never occur to him just to go take a nap. In very young children, many, many discipline problems can be avoided by simply knowing what *your* child's limitations are. Some toddlers can stay up late to greet the guests. Some just can't.

Another thing that toddlers and two year olds are almost completely unable to cope with is sharing. They've only recently acquired the understanding that something that is taken away from them doesn't disappear; at this age they cannot understand that what is removed from their hands still belongs to them. For a child who is just learning that he is a separate and unique person—able to have his own toys and able to say no—sharing can be overpowering and threatening. You can expect that toddlers will become upset about other children touching their toys. Expecting them to be "nice" to other children is mostly futile although it is best to *suggest* that they be nice so that they experience your standards of empathy and behavior. Meanwhile, try to distract them with something else when they become angry (even enraged) at a playmate. Children of this age should not be allowed to work things out for themselves. This is likely to lead to blows, and the children will learn nothing from that.

It is terribly important for the parents of toddlers to understand that a number of things that we might consider abnormal or neurotic in adults (or older children) are quite normal in the two- and three-year-old toddler. Many types of fear and anxiety—fear of being alone, terror of the dark, and discomfort at meeting new people—are really quite understandable, once we know something about their emotional and intellectual development.

As they grow older and become more mobile, more independent, and more verbal, toddlers' worlds become more complex. Two year olds, particularly, are often gripped by angers and hostilities strong enough to frighten them. Some psychologists believe that these negative feelings become transformed into the "monsters" that kids imagine lurk under beds and in their closets when it's time to go to sleep. Knowing that your child is *really* afraid and that this is not just an excuse to stay up later can help you help your child get some sleep. Leaving a light on may do the trick for some kids. Some parents buy the child an especially tough-looking stuffed animal to be the "night bear" to stand guard at the foot of the bed. Some parents find that music helps. The important thing is that parents take their kids' needs seriously and work with them to overcome the problem.

If the problem won't go away, it may be a clue that something else is upsetting your child. Think about what may be angering, frustrating, or otherwise stressing him during the day and see if you can help him put it into words. Listen carefully to what he *does* say and paraphrase his words to help him articulate more precisely what he is trying to communicate. (This "reflective listening" is discussed in detail in chapter 4.)

Most toddlers have what are often called "temper tantrums." The word *temper* suggests that these frightening displays of crying, screaming, and flailing are brought on by anger. But actually it is not so much anger, at least not in the sense that adults experience anger, as it is frustration.

As Dr. Lawrence Balter points out in his book *Child Sense*, frustration is a way of life for toddlers. Two and three year olds cannot understand why there are so many things that they cannot have or do. All day long, they climb on things that they have to get down from, they reach for things they can't have, and they are called away from things that beckon temptingly. This frustration is very stressful, and the resulting tantrums are a form of physical release from all that stress.

The intensity of tantrums can be scary. T. Berry Brazelton recounts that the first time one of his daughters had a tantrum, he thought she was having a convulsion, and he was terrified. What can you do when your child is having a tantrum? If he really gets out of control, you must restrain him or move him to a place with a soft rug. However, most children stop short of hurting themselves—they've still got a tiny bit of self-control lurking under all that fury. Dr. Balter notes that it can actually be sort of funny to watch a child peek at you out of the corner of his eye during his tantrum to see whether you think he's really going to bash his head against the wall. If he is, you must intervene, of course, but if he's not, the best thing you can do is to walk away, telling him that you'll talk with him when he's finished.

One aspect of tantrums that most disturbs parents is the fact that many children don't mind in the least letting it all hang out in public. In fact, most tantrums happen in places such as supermarkets and banks where children are bored and frustrated, and your attention is turned to what you have to do and they are surrounded by temptations. Sometimes it may be possible to avert a tantrum by distracting your child or by giving in or compromising. In the market, for instance, you can give a child a few items to look for and collect for you. Or you can agree in advance to one treat that the child knows he can have when the shopping's finished. If your child insists on having something you don't want to buy, decide if this is worth going (literally) to the mat for. If you cannot avoid the tantrum, it may be best to pick up the child and walk out. You can try again later or the next day.

But wait, you say, there are times when certain things

just have to get done. This is true, but it is probably less true, less often, than we think it is. For example, doing the grocery shopping at 6 p.m. on your way home from picking your child up from the day-care center is going to be tough. Your kid will be hungry and tired and will want your undivided attention. If you must shop, plan a strategy that takes his hunger into account (bring crackers and juice), his fatigue (limit your shopping list), and his need for you (involve him in what you are doing). If the child is just too tired, why push the situation until it becomes destructive to him—and to you? If there's really nothing to eat in the house, it might be the night to send out for pizza. The most important thing to remember about toddlers is that they are not toddlers forever. It's not always going to be like this.

By the way, it cannot be stressed too often that growth is a very individual, changeable thing. Some completely normal children will have tantrums at four years of age; sometimes a child who hasn't been afraid of snakes under the bed for years suddenly won't touch his foot to the floor (possibly after the birth of a sibling or some other stressful event). There is no substitute for knowing your own special child.

Preschoolers

As children grow up, their worlds expand: They go more places; they know more people; they have friends. Their relationships with others are more varied.

Children between three and five continue to reach out and explore the world. As they begin to experience their increasing autonomy, they yearn to be in control even more. Their frustrations are still intense, but their sense of accomplishment is intense, too. According to child psychologist

Lawrence Balter, the most often repeated expression of this age-group is "Watch me, Mommy!"

Not surprisingly, the greatest underlying developmental issue of the preschool years is independence. Therefore we have to accept that an enormous amount of what psychologists call "oppositional behavior" is normal. Oppositional behavior runs the gamut from shouting constant noes! and I won'ts! to dawdling when you're rushing out, refusing to wear the clothes you pick out, and wanting to eat only cream cheese and jelly sandwiches. The long and short of it is that all of this is behavior that demonstrates the child's autonomy. Autonomy is a crucial part of normal development, yet constant resistant behavior cannot possibly—and should not—be tolerated by parents. Luckily, along with this new autonomy comes an even greater desire to please parents and win their approval.

This can make it very difficult to know how to discipline preschoolers in a way that is effective but still appropriate. As aptly stated in *Dr. Balter's Child Sense;* "We want our children, in the long run, to be leaders, critical in their thinking, to have good judgement and a strong character. But in the short run, in our day-to-day life, we want children who will not talk back to us."

This problem is compounded by the fact that to a child at this age, almost every parental don't! strikes at that new and precious independence. Probably the best way we have of negotiating between healthy independence and the compliance necessary to children's safety and development is to establish good routines.

Routines

Routines—of waking, dressing, eating, sleeping, etc.,—are the structural foundation of a young child's day and, in many instances, of his life. Routines function constructively for children in a number of ways.

- Routines give a child a sense of security and stability. Doing (as much as possible) the same thing at the same time in the same way every day leaves the child emotionally free and safe to experiment and explore during the rest of his day. And this is precisely what preschoolers need to do.
- Routines serve the purpose of spelling out exactly what parents expect, when they expect it, and how they expect it. This is a clear advantage in avoiding discipline problems, and in applying discipline measures when necessary, because the child already *knows* what he should do.
- Routines teach certain concepts such as timeliness and order, for example, that we brush our teeth *after* we eat and *before* we go to bed, and that the building blocks always go back into the box after playing with them. You can see how children who are already familiar with these concepts have an easier time with such things as toilet training and, later, with the structure needed to succeed in school.
- Routines lead to a feeling of mastery for children. Day after day, they gradually learn to do things that they want and need to know how to do. Conflicts are lessened and kids can feel good about themselves.

Many parents find that it is easiest to start good routines, for example, bedtime procedures, when their children are toddlers. This is probably a good idea, although parents should be reasonable about how much regimenting such a young child can absorb.

However, it is never too late to start to establish good routines. The keys are gradualness, reasonable expectations, and consistency.

What if you really never got a bedtime routine going when your child was still a toddler? If you let him fall asleep at different times, in your arms, with or without his bottle, it's more difficult to get him to go to bed by himself at a reasonable hour and stay there. He may be going to bed so late that he's tired and grouchy in the morning, making him late for nursery school and making you worried that he isn't getting enough sleep.

A child who has been rocked to sleep, or nursed to sleep, or allowed to drop off in front of the television has learned to associate going to sleep with those activities. This makes it incredibly difficult for him to go to sleep in any other way. It is, in effect, a problem of having established the *wrong* routine.

In *Solve Your Child's Sleep Problem*, Dr. Richard Ferber, a pediatrician and expert in sleep, outlines a behavioral approach to reconditioning your child's sleep associations.

You've got to decide on a nighttime routine (ask your child what he would like)—let's say, 15 minutes of talking with you in bed and two stories. Then you have to *stick to it*. After the two stories, give him a kiss and tell him you'll be right out there in the living room, but that he must go to sleep.

If your child cries, let him cry for a predetermined length of time (say, 10 minutes), then go in and check him. Reassure him that you are right there, that you love him, but that he must go to sleep. Don't let him get out of bed if you can help it. Then leave. If he cries, wait 20 minutes before going in again. Repeat the procedure until he goes to sleep. Most children will settle themselves within a relatively short period of time—about a half hour. And most children will adapt to such a program in less than a week. Obviously the older the child, the longer he has had to form inappropriate routines and the longer it will take to form appropriate ones.

Sleep routines are good models for all types of routine because it is fairly easy for us to empathize with a child's need for them. Adults usually have some form of minimal routine they follow to get to sleep, without which they can feel out of sorts.

An example of another productive routine would be a sequence for getting dressed and getting out of the house in the morning. Marion, a Boston mother, says her 4¹/₂- and 2¹/₂-year-old boys know they must be dressed by the time *Mister Rogers* comes on the television. If they are not ready to go by then, they miss the chance to choose what they want for breakfast and have to eat a bagel in the car. Some mornings, she adds, this is just fine with them.

Marion's flexibility within the structure of the routine (it's not a punishment to eat breakfast in the car, just another choice) makes it easier for her children, and herself, to accept the routine and stick to it.

Sexuality

Along with the drive for independence and competence, the preschool years are the time when children begin to really experience and explore their sexuality—physically, emotionally, and intellectually. A child knows that he or she is a boy or a girl, and the difference between the two is usually of enormous interest.

Infants will explore their bodies with their hands and discover the pleasure they can give themselves when they touch their genitals, but it is not usually until a child is out of diapers that he begins to really be conscious of, and have access to, these parts of his body.

Let's say it once and for all: Masturbation is an entirely normal part of childhood. Children need to feel good about themselves and their *whole* bodies. If we give them the message that certain parts of their bodies are something to be ashamed of, they will have problems later on.

It is best to deal with masturbation in a matter-of-fact way. If the child is touching himself in public, just say, "Not here." Give him something else to do with his hands. Most children aren't really conscious of when they are playing with themselves and can be easily distracted.

The emotional dimensions of a child's sexuality can be equally disconcerting to parents. Because a preschooler's desire to be grown-up is even stronger than a younger child's and because he has many skills that younger children don't, he will make very determined efforts to be just like you, including emulating your role as a husband or wife. This is the time that little girls want high heels and lipstick and boys want to shave. It is also the time when boys want to marry Mommy and girls want Dad all to themselves.

It is terribly important to be sensitive to these desires, because what the child is really doing is trying out his own identity. Again, a matter-of-fact but loving approach is best ("I know you love me, honey, and I love you, too. When you're grown-up you'll have a girlfriend—but I'll always be your Mom"). One mother says that her middle son, Chris, told her that he would agree to marry one of his friends (instead of her), but that they would live in the attic while Mom lived downstairs. It can be quite poignant to see how preschoolers yearn to grow up and yet remain babies at the same time.

Helping Them Grow

Parents can aid and take advantage of a preschooler's desire to grow up by gradually increasing the responsibilities expected of him. Three to five year olds can certainly help clean up, dust, set tables, and help you with younger siblings. In fact, the most authoritative study on the relationships of brothers and sisters, "Siblings" done in England in 1982, showed that children whose mothers involved them in the care of their younger brother or sister developed a better relationship with their siblings. Responsibility will be one of the major themes for discipline in the school-age years, so it is wise to start thinking about it now.

School-Age Children

Going to school is, in effect, a child's definitive entrance into society. At school, all he has learned about relating to other people will be tested, explored, and expanded. Not surprisingly, many of the discipline issues that arise during these years have to do with how children get along with others as individuals and how they fit in with a group.

Psychologist Erik Erikson writes that the overwhelming "developmental task" of this age-group is to develop a feeling of industry and usefulness as opposed to inferiority and futility. In order to do this, children need not only to acquire skills, but to acquire skills that are *recognized and esteemed* by his family, his peer group, and society.

As might be expected, the discipline issues that most often arise in these years involve peer pressure and the need to conform, problems at school, and the desire for increasing freedom and independence coupled with a still-naive perception of their own abilities. Older children can be a little like toddlers in that they often bite off more than they can chew. David, age 12, went with two other boys to set off a cherry bomb in his school's garbage dumpster. But after they had done it, David was upset and sorry and immediately called his mother. He hadn't been able to think through the seriousness of his actions *before* the event, and when he realized what he had done he was overwhelmed. His parents helped him to be honest with the school authorities and to make amends.

It is important to remember that age appropriateness also takes into account the fact that as children grow they are ready for increasing responsibility. Just as we shouldn't expect a four year old to be as mature as a 10 year old, neither should we allow a 10 year old to behave like a four year old, free from any real responsibility. It is fair and reasonable to expect preteens to understand curfews and other limitations and to be able to handle some of life's inevitable disappointments, such as not being chosen for a team.

The preteen years are a good time to expand your child's role in the family by giving him his own jobs, such as taking out the garbage every night or raking the lawn. He is learning that everyone has a unique role and job in this world. He needs to learn that others can depend on him. Children flourish when they gain a sense of responsibility, if the demands are not excessive and if his sincere efforts are not criticized. If you ask a five year old to help you fold the wash and then refold it, while criticizing his attempt, he will learn not to try. A discouraged child does not believe that his individual actions make a difference. Likewise, a preteen needs to feel that he is able and that his efforts are respected.

At this time, the importance of honest and fair discipline becomes even more apparent. If you say you are going to help fix your son's bike this Saturday and you don't, your child will feel justified in reneging on his own agreements. Furthermore, if you discipline the child in dominating ways ("Because I say so") instead of in logical ways that respect him ("Because in this family you are not allowed to go to a movie alone until you are 13"), you will encourage disrespect for authority and deviousness. Your children are watching you more closely than ever now; therefore, it is important to show them decent, loving, and respectful adult behavior.

A Good Fit at School

Naturally, one of the issues that most concern parents is how their children get along in school. What should be expected of children academically and socially? How can we tell if a seemingly academic problem is the fault of a too easy or too difficult curriculum, an insensitive or demanding teacher, or something within the child's control?

Most academic problems can probably be circumvented by choosing, as much as possible, the right school or the right program or teacher within the school. In this, as in everything else, the key is knowing your child.

Some children are just fine in the traditional academic environment and some children need something different. Many public schools now offer ungraded programs in which children of different ages and different grades work together. For a child who needs some time to mature, this can be a much more positive experience than being left back; some children, particularly creative ones, benefit from an environment that is less competitive than many traditional classrooms, one in which each person is encouraged to follow his own interests.

Ideally, there should be enough leeway for every child to be an individual in every classroom in every school. However, this is not the case. A poor fit between teacher and child or between the school's philosophy and the particular child calls for parental intervention, not only because it is so discouraging to the child, but because it may cause a child to be stigmatized by his peers or other teachers for the duration of his time there.

Today, many schools are advocating a "back to basics" program. This has been interpreted in many different ways by many different schools. Some noted educators such as Dr. David Elkind, author of *Miseducation,* worry that the greater reliance on standardized tests and rote learning can be harmful. Some children, of course, do need a fairly rigid structure to flourish; others, however, are damaged by it. It is up to parents to make sure that the school their child is in is the best place for him to learn.

You set the stage for your child's academic success by understanding his unique way of growing and his intellectual and developmental capacities as well as by providing an appropriate environment and appropriate expectations. Doing homework and conforming to reasonable academic standards is usually a matter of getting the right routine going. (For example, first a snack, then some relaxing, then homework, and *only* then television.)

A Good Fit Within the Group

Preteens are exposed to competition from without and within. Even in schools where a great effort is made to preserve an emphasis on the individual and his own unique growth, children just naturally notice themselves in terms of how others see them. They judge themselves according to their relationship to their peers, and see themselves as fatter, skinnier, better at math, worse at reading, faster runners, or more afraid of the pool rather than as simply good at math, for example.

Children this age need to acquire feelings of mastery and competence in dealings with their peers. The school-age years are those in which issues of bullying, passivity, gossip, and belonging come up. Because preteens have a new sensitivity as to how they are perceived by others, these years inevitably hold at least a few painful experiences in which they discover that they are not at the center of everybody's universe.

It can be extremely painful for parents when their child is not invited to a birthday party or is picked on by the class bully. It is wise to count to 10, or 20, or 100, if necessary, before saying anything. Children easily pick up on our distress and may interpret it to mean that their disappointment or hurt is an even bigger deal than they thought. At this age, children need parents who have a healthy dose of detachment, not coldness or deliberate noninvolvement ("You'll just have to work it out yourself") but loving, noninterventive concern ("Why do you think Max always picks on you? What do you think you could do about it?").

Wanting to belong brings other problems: Preteens want the same toys, clothes, and food that they see on television or that they think other children have. Begging for things that you consider too expensive or otherwise inappropriate is common; stealing is also not entirely uncommon. Neither is lying. While these activities cannot be condoned, the consequences of these behaviors must involve the child's respect. He needs an opportunity to regain your trust. He does *not* need to feel like he's a terrible person, just that his *actions* are unacceptable.

Perhaps the biggest challenge to parents faced with discipline issues in this age-group is to help children communicate their feelings adequately in words. The tantrums and acting out of the preschool years are just not appropriate now, yet if children do not know how to express their jealousies, their frustrations, their envies, and their anger in words, those feelings will work themselves out in other, inappropriate, behaviors. It is a rule of thumb that a *chronic* misbehavior points to an underlying stress, anger, or other concern that needs to be brought to the surface.

It should come as no surprise that as children grow up, the key to healthy and harmonious relationships with them is the same as it is with adults: good communication. Good communication does not necessarily come naturally. It is a series of skills that any motivated person can learn and which will be discussed in detail in chapter 4.

What We Should *Not* Expect from Our Children

One of the most important things to come out of years of research into the developmental approach to discipline is the recognition that certain things simply are not disciplinary issues. Control over the bodily functions of eating, sleeping, and eliminating should be forever stricken from the list of parent-child conflicts and relegated to the developmental realm just like walking and talking.

Just as we would not dream of punishing a child because he keeps falling down as he is learning to walk or because he cannot pronounce words correctly the first time he babbles, we should not punish a child because he has only a fleeting understanding that the sensations in his bladder or lower intestines mean he is about to have a bowel movement or because he is not hungry when we want him to be.

If you are at loggerheads with your child over what and how much he eats, over wetting his pants or his bed, or not falling asleep at the hour you have chosen, these are battles that you don't have to win. You don't even have to fight them.

These issues become conflicts when *parents* make them into conflicts. But stop and think: Can anyone make *you* have a bowel movement if you're not ready or when you don't want to? No one can control anyone else's body. Attempts to do so will only lead to frustration and fighting in childhood and more serious problems later on. Many adult eating disorders have their roots in childhood battles over what, when, and where to eat and over the significance of eating. In the end, your child eats, sleeps, or makes a bowel movement because he needs to in order to live not to please you, thwart you, or because he is a genius or a brat.

Most normal children will naturally eat as much as they need and when they need. If you make good choices available in reasonable quantities at reasonable times, they will take care of themselves.

Jane Hirschmann and Lela Zaphiropoulos, coauthors of *Are You Hungry?*, point out that many of the ways parents control their child's eating contribute to the child losing contact with his own sense of hunger and fullness. Cleaning the plate, having to eat set portions of food, having to eat at certain times (different children handle this differently), having to eat things they don't like, all make children eat for reasons other than hunger. A common expectation such as making a child eat all his vegetables or meat before he can get dessert, they observe, only serves to make sweets more appealing and probably to make children consume more than they need or want.

Hirschmann and Zaphiropoulos suggest that when children ask for food, adults should respond: "Are you hungry?" This simple question will reveal that often children want attention, are tired, or don't like what they're supposed to eat. You can then give your child what he really needs and avoid using food for inappropriate purposes—a principal cause of weight problems.

The same is true for sleeping. *All* children will eventually put themselves to sleep. You can put them to bed, but you cannot, short of drugging them or knocking them senseless, make them go to *sleep*. It is important to help children get enough sleep, however, and often we must help our children get themselves to sleep. T. Berry Brazelton writes that nothing is sadder than seeing parents let a toddler wind himself into a frenzy because he is overtired and cannot calm himself down.

Let your child help you fashion a tranquil bedtime routine, and then make every effort to stick to it. Do not let your child wheedle his way into a different routine every night. The sameness of the sleep routine is really a type of autohypnosis; it actually makes the child sleepy.

Naturally, you should never use going to bed or going to sleep as a punishment. For suggestions on how to help your child settle down at bedtime, see chapter 5.

The most recent research in child development shows that it is not only futile to start toilet training before a child is ready, but it can actually be damaging. Children who are made to feel anxious or pressured about going to the bathroom often withhold feces or urine. This can lead to accidents, which are distressing to them and irritating to parents. It can also lead to constipation, which then makes it so painful for the child to eliminate that he holds it in even longer and exacerbates the problem. There are a number of signs of readiness for toilet training, which include:

- An interest in parents or siblings going to the bathroom.
- The ability to indicate to you when he had made or is going to make a bowel movement.
- Discomfort after soiling in a diaper.
- An understanding of the words for going to the bathroom, making a bowel movement, etc.
- The ability to use the words listed above.
- The ability to imitate you or others.
- An awareness of your feelings and a desire to please you.
- The ability to remove underpants or a diaper by himself.

It is well to remember that the overwhelming developmental task of the toilet-training age is independence and mastery. When you try to establish control over your child's biological functions you are at war with his development. If, for instance, your child occasionally urinated on the floor out of sheer defiance and the urge to be "oppositional" and independent by showing that only *he* is in control of his urine, you would probably be wise not to make a big deal out of it. It is when a child knows that your feelings are out of proportion to the act that he may continue to test you. It's very human: A typical response to someone trying to control us is for us to try to control that person. Nobody likes to feel out of control.

It should go without saying that children are more than amply motivated never to wet or soil themselves or their beds. It is not fun to wet your clothes in front of your friends or to wake up in a soaking bed, and it is horribly humiliating the older the child gets. Do not make it worse by judging your child. Instead, help him learn to change his clothes and his sheets himself in private and reassure him that as he grows this *will* go away. Bed-wetting is common even up to adolescence, especially in boys. In the infrequent cases where it persists past the age of 13, it can be treated with medication. It is *never* a matter of right and wrong.

Learning to attend to our bodies' own signals is one of the most important keys to lifelong health; it is a great gift to give your children. If you are embroiled in the losing proposition of trying to control your child's biology, give up. You'll both win.

In the end, we can expect that our children are going to watch us very carefully. What they see us do every day is much more important than what we tell them to do. We can very definitely expect children to take their cues from us: If we say one thing and do another, they will not miss it.

We hope that our children will preserve the moral, cultural, and religious values that we live with. But we have no guarantee of this. Children who see their parents practicing what they preach have the best chance of becoming adults who respect and carry on their parents' traditions. If we want little boys to grow up into husbands and fathers who feel a responsibility equal to their wives' for child care and housework, fathers will have to serve as positive role models. If we want children who love learning, we would do well to forgo the VCR occasionally and show them that books are a constant part of our lives, too. Living according to our own standards is the best way to teach children what we expect of them.

Children are always changing because they are always growing. It can be hard to keep up with their changes and hard to change our own expectations to fit their increasing maturity and growth. What worked yesterday may not work tomorrow (it might not even work later today!). We should expect that sometimes the lines will get crossed and kids will misbehave—just because they are healthy, growing kids and they have to test the waters. It can be hard to remember, too, that as your kid is testing the waters, he still needs you to pull him in when he's in danger of going overboard.

CHAPTER THREE

......

How Can We Be Effective Parents?

When I was in college, I had very strong ideas about what kind of parent I would be," says Linda, a nutritionist, and mother of Jenny, age three, and Larry, age seven. "I was never going to let my kids watch trashy stuff on television—maybe I even thought *my* kids wouldn't want to. Now, on weekend mornings, my husband and I are so desperate to sleep and the kids get up so early that we can't wait until that first cartoon hits the screen. Some nights, too, I let them stay up and watch things I don't particularly approve of because it's just so great to have an hour of quiet time with my husband.

"I'm not very consistent about how much and what they can watch, so half the time, when I decide they shouldn't see a particular program, they act as if they're being sent to jail. I probably give in too often, but frankly I think it's better than screaming at them like a shrew because I need a little more time to myself. This way, evenings are fairly pleasant.

"Screaming is the one thing I hate to hear myself doing. I think, 'That's it! I'm turning into my mother!' I always told myself I would be completely different when *I* was a mother; I was going to be perfect—ha, ha."

Growing into Parenthood

Probably the one thing we can count on from parenthood is that it is often quite different from what we had expected. Just as our children are capable of surprising us, we are capable of surprising ourselves. We may have thought that when *we* became parents we would not nag, scream, or threaten, or that *we* were always going to be calm and reasonable. But experience soon proves us wrong.

Probably no other human endeavor produces so much guilt as the day-to-day demands of parenting—demands that change just when we thought we were getting things under control. Many parents work outside the home for many hours each day, and this adds to the psychological pressure. We're told lately that spending "quality time" with our children is no longer good enough, but no matter how much time we spend with our kids, it either feels like not enough or too much. We're often needlessly hard on ourselves. Things work well most of the time, which is something we rarely stop and give ourselves credit for.

As we discussed in the previous chapter, the essence of a harmonious parent-child relationship is the "good fit"—the happy meeting of our expectations with our child's abilities. Because children are all individuals, and because they continually change as they grow, there are as many ways to be a good parent as there are children.

The Perils of Perfectionism

Because growth is so elastic, nothing gets in the way of finding a good fit like perfectionism. As parents, we sometimes pressure ourselves to be perfect, and we evaluate ourselves in terms of what others will think. Because of this we may focus on results and not on what it takes to achieve results. And we may become discouraged because things just about never go as well as we wish. We may find it very hard to remember that children aren't 2 or 7 or 10 forever— and that time does tend to make things better. We may find it hard to let go of the limits we have set for our children, because it may feel like things will really get out of hand if we're not personally on top of the situation at all times (even though we know, deep down, that no one can be).

What's really sad is that the discouragement we feel as parents is the same discouragement we felt as misunderstood children—and now, unfortunately, we are passing it on to *our* children. But if it's more or less the way we were programmed, how can we pull out the plug and reprogram ourselves?

A key concept in motivating change in our children's behavior is understanding that we cannot bring about *drastic* change. We can, and must, help them to improve some *behaviors,* but we must recognize that no one can actually change another person. We can only change ourselves. What this means is that the *only* way we have of changing our children's behavior is by coming to terms with our own.

Luckily, we have the greatest motivation in the world: our children. We also have our heartfelt desire—not to be perfect parents, but to be as good as we can be.

Being as good as we can be is a reasonable, *realistic* desire. Realistic expectations for parenting are based foremost on two things: understanding ourselves and understanding our children.

Know Thyself

Being realistic about parenting means giving ourselves some of the same slack we give our kids. First of all, it involves accepting our physical limitations. Parents can get cranky and overtired, too. If you were up twice during the night with a teething baby, you can expect to be out of patience with a kid who's just being a kid—whether he's a four year old in the "why?" stage, or a 10 year old who is in the throes of a passion for heavy metal played one decibel below the pain threshold. If your job requires you to deal with demanding people all day long, you can count on being less than receptive to your children's heightened need for your attention the moment you walk in the door.

We need to acknowledge our own needs—to say "Give me a few minutes alone, okay?"—to adequately attend to our childrens' needs. Acknowledging our needs does not mean putting ourselves ahead of our children. It just means not losing touch with our feelings, so that we are not tempted to act out our frustrations and other feelings in the ways that adults, just like children, sometimes do.

Communicating our feelings to our children can be just as beneficial as helping them to communicate their emotions to us. Even preschoolers can empathize with hunger, tiredness, and anger at someone (like the plumber who didn't show up when he was supposed to). As long as we don't burden children with confidences or emotional needs that are inappropriate (such as things that would make the child feel put upon, frightened, or insecure), children appreciate being told what their parents feel. It makes them know that they are valued and it lets them know their similar feelings are normal.

As parents, we may also be limited by temperament just as our children are. Carin, a writer and mother of twin nine-year-old boys, just cannot stand noise; her sons eventually learned that one of their mother's cardinal rules was that they save their most boisterous behavior for the backyard. Arnold, an accountant with an eye for detail and the ability to stay with a task for hours on end, found it hard to adjust to his four-year-old daughter's need for many different kinds of activities. He even wondered if she were hyperactive. But lots of stimuli and change was as natural to his daughter's age, development, and temperament as it was alien to her father's. Once he learned that this was an important aspect of her development and personality, he was able to be more tolerant.

Not only do we bring to the parent-child relationship our own individual personalities and abilities, we also bring our histories, our individual experiences, and, in particular, our childhoods.

Perhaps one reason we tend to set impossible standards for ourselves as parents is that within all of us lurks the child we once were. We retain, sometimes consciously, sometimes unconsciously, the records of having been sent to our rooms or spanked when we shouldn't have been, having been asked to do something we just didn't know how to do, or not asked to do something we desperately longed to show off. Somewhere inside us is the child who, with lower lip trembling, swore that she would never, *never* do the same thing when she had a child.

How We Develop Our Parenting Styles

Being a parent puts us in touch with our own childhoods as nothing else can. It does this in some very rewarding ways. For instance, seeing through a child's eyes makes us fresh; it reawakens the curiosity and delight we felt when everything was new. Taking a child to the beach for the first time becomes a rich, sensual experience for us as well as for the child.

But being a parent can also take us back to feelings of powerlessness and frustration that we once knew—whether we felt that way because our parents were overly punitive, indifferent, or both. It is probably best to accept that parenthood makes *everyone* feel somewhat like a child again, and that if we are willing, we can learn a lot about ourselves from our children.

One of the things children are quick to teach us about ourselves is how we respond to feelings of anger. (Anger, both parent's and child's, is also discussed in detail in chapter 7.) If, as children, we were not allowed to show anger—for example, if the adults in our family were made uncomfortable by conflict—then we may have trouble dealing with our anger toward our children. We may feel guilty when we are angry and therefore permit children to continue upsetting behaviors until we can't stand it anymore and blow up at them. If we were often not allowed to "own" and express our feelings (of jubilation, rage, sadness, envy, or whatever) a related problem may occur: We may not even know exactly what our feelings are in a given situation. As a result, we may allow our children to transgress our limits until we lose our tempers. Some parents who would describe their parenting style as "permissive" may recognize themselves in these scenarios.

Often parents who were brought up very strictly them-selves find it difficult to accept the intense, defiant anger of their children and become convinced that stern measures are necessary. They may be threatened by the prospect of either themselves or their children being out of control be-cause as children such loss of control would have brought punishment. They may also have a need to feel respected by the child as they were not respected as children.

It is easy to see how both "authoritarian" parenting and "permissive" parenting can lock us in a vicious circle. With a permissive parent, the children go further and further each time to find the parent's limits. After each traumatic blowup, the child feels more confused and more insecure and more in need of testing the parent. With an authoritar-ian parent, the child rebels against too rigid rules or fights off punishment. The parent then believes that it is neces-sary to become even tougher.

If you find that you don't get angry until you just can't take it anymore and then you blow up and say or do things that you regret, you may have backed yourself into an overly permissive style. If you find that you often feel locked into power struggles with your child ("She did that just to get back at me") or that occasionally you feel it necessary to "put her in her place" with a well-aimed put-down, you may be trapped in an authoritarian mode. Actually, most of us tend to vacillate between both poles, which is confus-ing for children and ultimately ineffective for us as parents.

What can we do if we find ourselves acting in ways that we don't like, such as nagging or hitting? Or what if we find ourselves acting in ways that we simply feel are un-productive? We derive our parenting styles from the homes we grew up in (and sometimes our parenting styles are a reaction *against* what we knew at home). But just because we grew up with something, that doesn't mean we have to stick with it if we are unhappy with it. We can keep what was good and change what could have been better. We can take a good look at ourselves and set about deliberately becoming the kind of parent we really want to be.

The authoritarian and permissive parenting styles have been identified by Diana Baumrind of the University of California at Berkeley as among three principal disciplinary styles. The third, and most successful, is the "authoritative" style. Parents who espouse this style are more likely than permissive or authoritarian parents to have children who learn self-control and self-reliance. These children are also more confident and at ease in their daily interactions.

What Is Authoritative Parenting?

Authoritative parenting means setting firm and consistent limits; *and also* being warm and respectful toward the child. Authoritative parenting is thoughtful. It might not come naturally at first; it requires taking a little time to think before you act. But you don't have to have been brought up by ideal parents in order to treat your own children authoritatively. Adopting this parenting style simply requires a willingness to learn to:

- Tailor expectations to your child's developmental abilities.
- Remember that children model their behavior on that of their parents.
- Teach thinking skills by offering reasons for your requests and choices within your demands.
- Help children to negotiate for what they want.

Authoritative parenting is also fair, letting children experience the logical consequences of a behavior rather than expecting a punishment. For instance, Jared refused to put his new bicycle into the backyard shed after he used it. His father held back on his impulse to do the chore himself and let the bike sit outside. That night it rained and Jared woke up the next morning to find the new padded leather seat waterlogged. Through his father's nonintervention, Jared was forced to face the direct results of his behavior.

Who "Owns" the Problem?

One method that authoritative parents can use to solve a problem is to decide who *owns* the problem. Don Dinkmeyer, Ph.D., and Gary D. McKay describe this approach in their work, *The Parent's Handbook: Systematic Training for Effective Parenting (STEP)*. "Owning the problem" means figuring out who suffers the *immediate* negative consequences of a bad behavior: who is frustrated or upset right now, as opposed to who may or may not develop a problem down the road. Asking who owns the problem is a key to knowing how to deal with it.

For example, Marisa likes to borrow things such as scissors, adhesive tape, and glue from her mother's desk. Unfortunately, she often neglects to return them and occasionally forgets where she left them. The person who experiences immediate distress here is Marisa's mother, because it is she who is inconvenienced by not having the things she wants when she needs them. When Marisa's mother asked herself how to solve this problem, she felt that she needed to (1) prevent Marisa from taking her things and (2) tell Marisa how much this upset her.

If Marisa had been a preschooler, it would been a good idea for her mother to make sure that Marisa had her own plastic scissors and other appropriate materials so that she wouldn't have to borrow Mom's. But because Marisa is 10 years old, she is old enough to deal with the logical consequence of this behavior: not being allowed to use her mother's things next time she wishes to do so. She is also old enough to understand and empathize with her mother's distress over her possessions. After all, Marisa has lots of personal things she cares about, too.

Another kind of problem that often is owned by a parent is that of inappropriate activities in the house. Five-year-old Roxanne had three friends over, and they were sitting on the living room rug, coloring with magic markers in their coloring books. Roxanne's mother was concerned about the rug becoming stained, so she offered Roxanne a choice: Either she and her friends take the markers into Rox's room or they spread newspapers under their coloring books and color with crayons, which aren't as indelible.

An example of an issue that is owned by the *child* is the common problem of children who cannot get themselves ready on time. The logical consequence of such behavior could be missing an outing that the child really wants to go on. If the problem is getting to school on time, let the child experience the consequences of being late (it's wise to call ahead to the school and explain what's going on). If the child misses her bus, let her walk. If walking would be unsafe or the school is too far away, the authors of the *STEP* handbook suggest two solutions:

1. Change the morning routine. Let the child know that if she wants breakfast she must be ready to leave before she comes to the table. If she takes too long, breakfast gets packed off with her that morning.
2. If there is a parent or other care giver at home, let the child stay home, but limit her activities as though she were staying home for the appropriate reason of being sick. No television, no playing outside, no seeing her friends after school, etc. Do not get into conversation or

play with the child. Most children find moping around with nothing to do for one day so boring that they are fairly motivated to speed themselves up the next morning.

In some cases, excessive dawdling may indicate a problem at school. Usually, you'll be able to distinguish tardiness from reluctance to face difficult issues with teachers or peers. If you feel that your child's dawdling is, indeed, the result of some rocky roads at school, make a special effort to let her know you're ready to listen to her problem if she wants to talk. You may also want to consider setting up an appointment with your child's teacher.

The Power of Choice

Parents can also ask their children to come up with their own choices in solving problems. Twelve-year-old Raquel's father was tired of her always tying up the phone in the evenings, so he asked her to find ways that would help her limit her phone use. She suggested that if she were allowed to stay out with her friends for another hour after school instead of having to come right home and do her homework, she wouldn't need to talk to them so often on the phone. Her father agreed with it. It may interest an older child to be informed that labor negotiations and other legal agreements often involve just such compromises, and that the success of these pacts relies on each side keeping its word.

Helping a child to learn how to compromise and negotiate for what she wants is another way of giving a choice. It is also an effective way to approach certain behaviors, for example, begging for expensive toys, wanting to stay up late, or not wanting to help around the house. Children who want you to buy things for them can be encouraged to do *extra* work around the house (not the ordinary chores expected of them) in order to earn the extra money. Children who want to stay up late may agree to do some part of their morning routine, such as make their own lunches, the night before. Children who don't want to do their fair share in the family need to understand that we *all* have our jobs. Older children can be impressed by thinking about what would happen if you refused to do *your* job, such as drive them somewhere or make dinner.

When authoritative parents give a child choices, they are still setting clear limits, but they are doing it in a way that casts no blame and allows the child to retain some mastery over his life. Giving choices actively involves the child in solving the problem—this makes children responsible and promotes their confidence in their own ability to work things out themselves. By basing these choices on an understanding of who owns the problem, parents can keep the focus on *the behavior* and not on *the person*—and, last but not least, they get the job done.

When to Take Unilateral Action

Sometimes, however, you just can't offer a child a choice. A behavior may be so inappropriate or dangerous that you can't risk the child repeating it. (Unacceptable behaviors are discussed in depth in chapter 6.) Or maybe the child is too young to understand the consequences (a toddler repeatedly goes for an electric outlet even though she has been cautioned often and in no uncertain terms) or old enough to ignore the consequences (a school-age child riding a bike in a busy street).

At these times, it is probably best to remove the child from the scene for an appropriate length of time to a place where he will be alone and think: a method called "time-out." Toddlers can be put in a playpen or sat down in a special chair; older children may be sent to their rooms or to a specially designated place (hallways are usually good—there's nothing to do there, but because they are centrally located kids see what they're missing).

In order for time-out to be effective, you should choose to use it with behaviors that your children understand are inappropriate according to your standards (running in the house or throwing things, for example). First, warn the child that she will be put in time-out if she persists in a behavior. Say it clearly and in advance of the situation. If she continues to misbehave, be sure to use time-out *immediately* after the unacceptable behavior. Tell the child why you are doing this and for how long you intend to do it. It's good to use a timer because to be removed from your and others' attention, and from all activity, is a heavy price for a child to pay.

Because this is such a meaningful penalty to a child, it is terribly important to be sensitive to the potential for abuse. Time-out does not mean giving the child the "silent treatment." It is extremely cruel not to speak to a child. In time-out, we refrain from speaking to the child only for a specified and appropriate length of time—usually one minute for each year of the child's age. For really serious behaviors such as riding a bike in a busy street, it may be appropriate to keep the child from playing outside for as long as a few days; this is not a time-out strictly speaking, but it is nonetheless a meaningful removal from the "scene of the crime."

Thoughtful Parents, Thoughtful Children

The methods used by authoritative parents all have one element in common: They encourage thinking. By definition, they require some forethought and deliberation. They are not knee-jerk reactions. In the end, the one thing we should be able to expect from ourselves as parents is that we think about who we are and what we are doing. We may not be able to go from a Type A overachiever to a mellow, easygoing sort or vice versa, but we can at least know ourselves and know what our limitations are. That is the only basis we have for figuring out effective solutions to the problems that arise in family life.

Interestingly, authoritative parenting methods also get children thinking. Children must make choices, devise alternatives, and actively figure out how to get what they want. Even time-out promotes thinking: As the child expends his anger, he usually calms himself and is amenable to reflection. Children will often, and fairly quickly, come to appreciate the inappropriateness of their actions, *if* we resist the temptation to lecture them. Small children need us to direct their efforts at reflection, but like all of us, they respond best if we discipline with restraint and sensitivity. Older children have greater degrees of self-awareness, although they still need us to be clear about what we expect from them.

Authoritative discipline relies on parental self-awareness. This self-awareness is in fact what we hope, ultimately, to impart to our children. We pray that toddlers learn never to run into the street when we're not there, and we hope that older kids do their homework on their own, brush their teeth, and take care of their pets. We want our children to grow up able to take care of themselves in all ways, not just in terms of safety, school, and grooming, but also spiritually and morally. We hope they will stand up for what they believe and be kind to themselves and to others.

In this respect, what matters is not only how we behave toward our kids but also how we behave toward each other. We are the most important teachers our children will ever have. What they are learning from us every day—every minute—isn't what to wear or how to succeed. It's how to live. If we live as much as possible according to the standards we expect from them, they will strive to do this, too. If we take care of ourselves, we give our children the greatest opportunity to learn to do the same thing. We cannot control the world our children live in. But if we are respectful toward each other, our children will have a hard time learning any other way to treat people. That's the bottom line.

We can't expect to be consistent all the time—we're not robots—but we can hope for the courage to try. It takes a lot of courage to be a good parent: courage to make mistakes and to try again the next day; courage to be honest with ourselves, not just with our children. We want so much to be nothing but terrific in their eyes, yet even our imperfections can be of benefit to our children, teaching them how to get along, with cheerfulness and dignity, in an imperfect world.

Although we are the most important teachers our children will ever have, in many ways, our children may be the most important teachers *we* ever have. They give us the opportunity to look back at our own childhoods and understand why we're the way we are, as well as provide us with the motivation to become the nurturing and competent adults we really want to be.

PART II

• • • • • •

Growing As a Family

"Parents are so inconsistent. First, they force you to go to bed. Then eight hours later, they force you to get up!"

CHAPTER FOUR

· · · · · ·

Learning How to Communicate Effectively

O nce when my daughter was eight, she was whining about everything in sight, so I told her to write me a letter,'' says Amy, a medical technician. ''I said, 'If you have complaints, put them in writing.' She knows that's what you do if there's a problem with the electric bill or something like that. So she did—and it was 10 pages long! Now she writes 'complaint' letters whenever she feels she's being treated unfairly. Some of her letters are so funny—I love them! I realized that when she was whining I couldn't stand listening to her, even though sometimes what was bothering her was perfectly reasonable.''

It's an old truth that what matters is not just what you say but how you say it. Finding the right words, the right context, the right time to say something is an integral part of getting a message across.

It would be easy if words automatically corresponded to actions or feelings and if everybody understood a given word used in a given way. But this, we know, is not so. It is the mystery that great literature is based on; it is also the basis for many misunderstandings between spouses and parents and children.

There can be no effective discipline without effective communication. In fact, in many ways good discipline is

71

simply the result of clear and consistent communication. Children can only meet their parents' expectations when they understand what those expectations are. In order to communicate effectively, both parties must be able to acknowledge the other's point of view and to recognize the other's needs and feelings. In addition, parents have the responsibility of learning how to "read" those children who—whether by age or by nature or because the subject is especially delicate—have a hard time putting things into words.

Inadequate communication can cause another serious problem for kids: When a child is troubled or angry or otherwise upset about something that he doesn't know how to put into words, he will tend to express his disturbance in other ways. This is exactly what we mean when we call certain unacceptable behaviors "acting out": The child is acting out his feelings rather than talking about them. Crankiness (as most adults well know) can be one of the body's responses to stress; so can nightmares, insomnia, and other sleep disruptions, which exhaust the child and therefore fuel the problem.

The week nine-year-old Noah's mother went back to work, he began picking fights with his seven-year-old brother. He was also somewhat withdrawn and surly toward his parents. His mother realized that even though Noah saw her only three hours less a day, the idea of her working was still something that Noah had to adjust to. He felt as though he was getting less of her attention. Noah's mother helped him to talk about his resentment and asked him to choose something that he would like them to do together on the weekend. The result: The trouble he'd been having with his brother dissipated because Noah's dialogue with his mother gave him the *attention* he craved. It also let him *express his feelings*, and it gave him something to plan over which he *could* have control. These are three wonderful benefits of clear communication.

Communication As a Learned Skill

In her book *Loving Your Child Is Not Enough*, Nancy Samalin tells about running into an old friend several months after she had studied parent–child communication techniques with Dr. Alice Ginott. After Samalin told her friend how deliberate changes in the way she now communicated with her kids resulted in much greater harmony at home, her friend was incredulous. ''You have to go to school to study how to talk to your children?'' she asked.

The truth of the matter is that making an effort to use a number of communication skills consistently *does* work and is worth the initial awkwardness you may feel as you try to change the way you talk to your children. Effective communication works between adults, too. If it didn't, companies would not pay hundreds of thousands of dollars to teach many of the same skills listed here to their managers and employees. Research has shown that when workers are spoken to and listened to with deliberation, respect, empathy, and consistency, productivity increases because, among other things:

- Everyone understands what the goals and expectations are.
- Grievances are not left to fester unexpressed.
- People feel valued when they are listened to.
- People are not afraid to ask questions and thus accomplish tasks faster and with fewer mistakes.

There's a common theme here: Good communication makes people feel better about themselves, and this makes everything easier. Children are human beings with many of the same needs as adults. What works for workers and managers can work for families, too. Indeed, such skills enriched by tender loving care work even better at home. And there's a certain momentum: When you're pleased with your child's behavior, he delights in your approval, and aims to please you even more.

Six Steps to Successful Communication

The six communication skills that will be discussed here have been around for a while. They are basic and proven. However, they are not mathematical formulas—no $E = mc^2$ and *Kaboom!* no more problem. They are more like recipes for brownies. Everybody has his own favorite, which he makes his own special way. Try these techniques in your own words and in your own style.

1: I-Statements

Discussed in chapter 1, I-statements are basic to the repertoire of effective communication. They are satisfying because you get to say what you feel when you, the parent, have a problem that the child might not think is a problem until you point it out. It's effective because you are saying what you feel without attacking anyone.

The fact that I-statements leave out the blame but focus on the behavior and the consequences of the behavior makes them clear to the child and easier for him to respond to. For example, three-year-old Martha wanders away from her mother in the mall. Ten minutes later, her frantic mother is notified by loudspeaker that her child is safe in the management office.

A typical response might have been to confuse the child by asking an unanswerable question ("How could you have wandered off?"), or to upset the child by showing intense anger when the child is already frightened. Neither response lets the child know explicitly what he did wrong, how you feel about it, and why.

Don Dinkmeyer and Gary D. McKay, in the *STEP* handbook, outline three steps in constructing an I-statement, which are applied below to the situation faced by Martha's mother.

1. Describe *the behavior:* "When you walked off by yourself . . ."
2. State *your feeling* about the consequence the behavior produces *for you:* "I was so worried that something happened to you . . ."
3. State the *objective consequence:* ". . . because I didn't know where you were."

Dinkmeyer and McKay also make the point that I-statements are flexible—you can make I-statements that don't include your feelings but merely delineate a behavior and its consequences: "I can't get the car out of the garage when your bike is in the driveway."

Part of what makes an I-statement valuable is what it *isn't.* It is not saying *"I'm* angry at you because *you* . . ." It's about you and your child's *behavior.* It is not about your child as a person. There's no room in an I-statement for sarcasm, ridicule, blame, or humiliation. If you attack your child with these weapons, however innocuous they may seem to you, your child will most likely respond to the attack rather than address himself to the behavior, when the latter is what you really want.

2: Reflective Listening

This is the art of helping a person to articulate his feelings in words by mirroring back to him what he is saying. This is an excellent technique when your child has a problem. For example, four-year-old Sonny comes in from playing in the yard and starts careening around the house, banging into things with his plastic army men.

MOM: You sound mad.

SONNY: I hate Larry! I'm never letting him come here again.

MOM: You're really upset with him.

SONNY: He's a doo-doo.

MOM: He must have really made you mad.

SONNY: Yeah, he always grabs all my men.

MOM: Maybe next time we can remind him to bring his own men with him.

SONNY: He can only come if he has his own men and doesn't touch mine.

Reflective listening such as this works with preschoolers because they cannot see cause and effect very clearly. They can benefit from a little help in straightening out the source of their anger. Older children face a different problem in putting their feelings into words: Their feelings may be more complex and occasionally painful. Take the case of 12-year-old Laurie:

LAURIE: I won't wear that pink dress to Grandma's! I can't stand it!

MOTHER: You liked it when I bought it *(Then, catching herself)*, but you sure seem to feel strongly about it . . .

LAURIE: It's awful.

MOTHER: It's awful?

LAURIE: It's too puffy. I want to wear the blue one—I look thinner in it . . .

By using reflective listening, Laurie's mother realized that Laurie was much more sensitive about her weight than she had imagined. After a few more minutes of letting her daughter do the talking, it emerged that one of her schoolmates told Laurie that she looked like a "tub" in her pink dress. Her mother decided that clothes were not a big enough issue for her to insist on if it was going to make Laurie feel bad about herself.

Reflective listening doesn't come easily. It takes discipline on the parent's part to really listen to what the child is saying and avoid interpreting, analyzing, or putting words into the child's mouth.

This technique is very useful in getting kids to *open up* rather than *act out*. Sometimes you can see that a certain behavior just cries out for attention. Listening reflectively provides the attention the child craves, and also puts the problem into words. Sometimes older kids catch on and get irritated ("You're just saying what I'm saying!"), but don't get dissuaded. The detachment of reflective listening—if practiced sincerely and lovingly—will eventually open a space for even the most difficult feelings to come out.

Another tip: Don't just listen with your ears, use your whole body. Watch for visual signs, facial expressions and gestures; put your hand lightly on the child if he seems receptive; try to get a "feel" for his feelings. It's the concentrated attention that reflective listening supplies as much as the verbal exchange that is so healing.

3: Acknowledging Feelings

If you make an effort to get a feel for your child's feelings, it will be much easier to acknowledge those feelings. Acknowledging feelings is very much like reflective listening, but its applications are different. Nine-year-old Frank found it very difficult to handle his disappointment when his soccer team lost a game. He would kick the wall or throw his soccer shoes. His father intervened by telling him clearly that he knew that it felt terrible to lose a game, *but* that Frank was not allowed to be destructive. This is much more effective than simply insisting that he stop showing his anger and disappointment.

In our adult lives, we respond well when our feelings are respected. If a friend calls you to say that he is going to be a half hour late, you take it much better than if he simply kept you waiting. Kids take discipline better when you acknowledge that what is happening may be uncomfortable for them, but explain why such measures are necessary.

True acknowledgment of feelings is not a superficial courtesy, sugarcoating the pill of parental direction or discipline. If you *say* that you know how something feels but you aren't truly focused on it at all, your child will unerringly know you are not really being empathetic. He will get the message that you feel it is okay to treat his feelings in a cavalier way. Real acknowledgment is nothing more or less than empathy: the ability to feel with someone else or to walk a mile in his shoes, as the saying goes. On a deeper level, all true communication relies on empathy, on the understanding that two people feel the same way about the same words.

The goal of empathetic communication is an important one in family life and in general. Empathy creates common ground, a context in which things are understood the same way by different people.

If your first reaction to a child's behavior is empathetic, it is likely that the child will be better able to respond to whatever change in behavior you request. You have seen the situation through his eyes, and are now inviting him to see it through yours. Empathy has this quality of reverberating back and forth between people; it is, in this sense, the ideal way to address behaviors that affect others.

Even very young children can respond to a degree to empathetic direction. For instance, Tina was having her second birthday party. When her mother put the cake down in front of her, Tina reached out a grabbed a handful of frosting, which she delightedly mushed into her mouth. "It feels good to squish the frosting, doesn't it?" Tina's mother said. "But if everyone did that, the cake would fall apart and there would be no more cake for anyone. Not for you, for me, or for anyone." Tina looked around at all the children and was able to wait until the cake was served to eat her share.

One note: Empathy is a powerful and natural emotion. It should never be used to make a child feel guilt that is out of proportion to the situation. It can be easy to manipulate children through guilt; this is very painful for a child and harmful in the long run.

4: Using Fantasy

Children have very good imaginations, and fantasy is still very much a part of their daily lives. Fantasy is a way of using imaginative ideas and language to solve real problems.

Fantasy can work wonderfully with young children in the

tantrum years because you may be able to distract them and keep them from locking in on their frustration, if your timing is good. For example;

LONNIE: I want another cookie.
DAD: You already ate three cookies; that's enough.
LONNIE: I want it!
DAD: How many more do you want? One? Five? Fifty?
LONNIE: A hundred!
DAD: Why not five hundred?
LONNIE: Fifty hundred . . .

With both older and younger children, fantasy can sometimes help to deal with problems that really have no solution. Nine-year-old Toinette missed her grandmother terribly after Grandma died, but she rarely said anything about it. One day when her mother noticed Toinette moping in her room, she asked her about it. Notice that the conversation begins with Toinette's mother merely listening reflectively to her daughter.

MOTHER: You look kind of sad. Are you feeling sad?
TOINETTE: *(Nodding without speaking)*
MOTHER: Can you tell me what makes you feel sad?
TOINETTE: I just feel sad.
MOTHER: Feeling sad really weighs you down.
TOINETTE: Yeah.
MOTHER: You can't help thinking sad thoughts over and over.
TOINETTE: I keeping thinking about Grandma.
MOTHER: Thinking about Grandma makes you feel sad, doesn't it? Sometimes when I miss Grandma I just think about what we would be doing right now if she were here. Like going shopping.

TOINETTE: Yeah. Grandma would have let me have that yellow bathing suit that you wouldn't let me have.

MOTHER: Probably. She'd let you wear eye makeup and drive a car. What else?

TOINETTE: She'd let me have everything you won't let me have. And I wouldn't have to do homework. And I wouldn't have to fold any stupid clothes for anyone. And . . .

MOTHER: You and Grandma would run the show . . .

The example above does not deal with a discipline problem per se, but a problem of unexpressed emotion. Using fantasy to help bring emotions into manageable form, however, is a very valuable way to prevent discipline problems.

Imagination is as important a faculty as our intellectual, emotional, and moral capacities. However, we tend to be so bound by dealing with reality that we don't afford ourselves the break that imaginative thinking can offer. Children's imaginations are more functional; they work with very little stimulus.

Fantasy can be one of the most rewarding kinds of communication to share with your children—one in which your child may give much more than he takes.

5: Humor

Humor should be self-explanatory, but actually it is rather easy to lose our sense of humor when we are dealing with a sullen child.

We lose our sense of humor when we become locked in to reacting. If you have ever watched a child ''lock himself in'' to a behavior—for example, refusing to take no for an answer when begging for a new toy—you know how suddenly nothing else in the world exists except the thing the child wants and cannot have. He doesn't remember all the toys he just got for his birthday a week ago. He doesn't remember that you're having his favorite meal for dinner. Nothing else matters.

In reacting to our children, we are easily locked in much in the same way. Our automatic responses cause us to lose perspective.

Humor is the great restorer of perspective. The ability to laugh, especially at ourselves, means that we can stand aside from a situation and appreciate it from another point of view.

Humor is personal and spontaneous; everyone has his own style. Even people who can never tell a joke are capable of coming out with something hilarious when the absurdity of a situation strikes them. And sometimes pointing out the absurdity of a situation encourages a resistant child to deal with it. Michael would not clean up his room, so his mother left him an effective note—from his socks: "Please put me in the laundry with all my friends. Thanks, Your Socks." This 30-second effort achieved what quite a few hours of nagging had not; Mike chuckled and dropped his socks into the hamper—along with the rest of their "friends."

It's impossible to teach someone how to be funny. We can only try to look on the light side of things. And remember that humor means laughing *with*—not *at*—someone. Ridicule and sarcasm have no place in our conversations with our children. Like physical abuse, such verbal taunting is not something children can bounce back from. It is overpowering and scary.

6: Model Dialogues

Model Dialogues are exactly what they sound like—dress rehearsals for real conversations that we feel we need to be prepared for.

Everyone knows at least one person with whom it is hard to talk: a boss, a client, an interviewer, sometimes even a family member. Conversations with that person tend to degenerate into arguments or you feel you don't get a chance to say what you want to say. You walk around for hours later, thinking, "If only I'd said A when he said B."

Once children are off to school, they are involved in a myriad of social relationships, some of which can be problematic. They can get picked on by bullies, excluded by snobby cliques, or repressed and stifled by a heavy-handed teacher.

In a model dialogue, a parent takes the role of the problem person (or very occasionally, and only as an example, the child) and both parent and child try out solutions in their new roles.

When Jimmy was being picked on by a tough boy in the fifth grade, his father and he tried out some scenarios:

FATHER: You look like a girl.
JIMMY: So do you.
FATHER: You're dumb, you don't know anything.
JIMMY: Neither do you.
FATHER: You're a jerk.
JIMMY: I'm rubber, you're glue; whatever you say bounces off me and sticks to you.

After they'd gone a few rounds, they started laughing. "It won't be that easy at school," Jimmy told his Dad. "I know it won't," his father acknowledged, "but at least

83

you'll have a few phrases ready.'' The extra support of his father's time and attention certainly didn't hurt when Jimmy had to contend with the bully next time.

Aggressive children who lose their temper easily can benefit from model dialogues, as well as more passive children who have a tough time sticking up for their rights.

A word of caution: Model dialogues are not an opportunity for you to direct the movie of your child's life. They are a chance for the *child* to come up with alternative ways of responding in situations that the child finds overwhelming. Your kid has got to do it himself—otherwise it's worse than not doing it at all. If Jimmy's father had come up with all the answers, then the next time the tough boy picked on Jimmy, he would have felt even more inadequate.

Communication skills need not feel forced or ''serious.'' In fact, there's almost an element of play in using them, and children usually respond well to a game when the rules are flexible enough to accommodate them. If you keep a light heart as you try out these methods, you will most likely find that what at first seemed awkward and stiff becomes very satisfying—and sometimes even fun.

CHAPTER FIVE

· · · · · ·

How to Avoid Everyday Battles

The tone of family life is not set by our staged philosophy of discipline. It is set by our responses to the million trivial daily demands of raising children—from the moment the kids wake up in the morning and choose some wretched outfit to wear to the moment the light in their bedroom finally goes out at night. The more predictable these responses are, the easier it is for children to reflect the behavior parents expect of them. This predictability is largely accomplished by setting up good routines, as discussed in chapter 2. Yet, even with good routines, every day brings its own surprises. Children are constantly growing and changing, and sometimes it can be difficult for adults to keep up.

For parents who want to create an atmosphere in which children learn self-discipline, the best responses are not nagging and yelling at them to do things your way. You can actively vary routines just enough to accommodate your child's particular needs at a given time. The suggestions outlined here require little more than that you try to stay relaxed and flexible. As we've seen, the best responses require an understanding of each child's stage of development, a recognition of each child's unique temperament, and a willingness to offer choices to even a young child. They also require a sense of perspective (every glass of milk is not a health issue) and the same kind of common sense that warns parents of toddlers to remove the china figurines from the coffee table *before* disaster strikes.

The Top Ten Battlegrounds— How to Find Peace

Below are 10 of the most frequent sources of everyday conflict (arranged alphabetically) between parents and children and some practical advice for handling them.

Baths

Most infants love their baths, but between the ages of one and two, some children become afraid of the water. They may not want to be handled or they may worry that they will lose their new, tenuous balance in the slippery tub. In any case, the fear is normal and is usually temporary. Meanwhile, bathe your child in a small plastic basin or, in the summer, try using a wading pool. Reintroduce the big tub by sharing a few baths there with your child or by filling it only slightly at first and gradually adding more water each time.

When children are older, you can add toys, bubbles, or even siblings (if they're agreeable to the arrangement) or friends to the bath for fun. Some parents make baths special by restricting indoor use of squirt toys and bubble blowers to the tub.

Older grade-schoolers who resist baths usually do so because they interfere with some other, more interesting activity. This resistance can be prevented by giving the bath a regular and nonnegotiable place in the schedule and by preparing the child (who is watching television or playing a game) in advance, giving her a chance to change gears. Some parents even use a kitchen timer, set five or 10 minutes before bath time, to warn that when the alarm goes off, it is time to pop out of clothes and into the tub.

In addition, all children have personal preferences for their baths—hot or cool, bubbles or no bubbles, company or no company, halfway full or almost overflowing, washcloth or sponge, boats or dinosaurs, cups or squeeze bottles. They like making those decisions themselves and having them respected.

Preteens require special handling when it comes to setting standards of cleanliness. Different kids will react differently to the changes that their bodies are undergoing. Some, for instance, may become uncomfortable about nudity and resist bathing for days on end. Others react in quite an opposite way—staying in the shower for an hour or more, twice a day. As with any other body-related issue, the important thing for parents to do is to respect the child's need for privacy, letting her know that she has reached a stage where taking care of her body is primarily her responsibility.

Bedtime

In some families bedtimes are a warm, cozy time of togetherness; in others they are a battle of wills. One of the best ways to avoid nightly nagging and fights is to establish a bedtime and stick to it. Relax your child about a half hour beforehand by winding down any highly stimulating activities. Because young children find rituals reassuring, many families establish them for bedtime—three stories; a glass of water, two songs, and a tape; fifty kisses and a hug. If you begin and end the ritual the same way each night, your child will know exactly what to expect once it starts. If you allow "one more" and "one more" and "one more," that will also become part of an endless routine.

Many children who resist going to bed would just rather be up with you or watching television. Other children are afraid of the dark or of being alone. Talk to your children about those fears and then offer them a night-light or something familiar to sleep with for comfort. If you think taking a favored toy or object to bed will become part of your child's nighttime ritual, you may want to plan ahead: Encourage your child to choose a special blanket or stuffed animal as a sleepmate.

A problem some parents encounter is that children's sleep needs do not always mesh with those of adults. If your child is just not tired at the established bedtime, you cannot force her to fall asleep. What you can demand is that she stay in bed and play quietly—with toy figures or books or stuffed animals. If you give an older child a flashlight or a reading light for these activities, you can turn off the overhead light and keep the room dark. In addition, she will have the opportunity to put herself to sleep in response to her body's need by turning off the light.

As much as preteens need sleep, they need to have their approaching maturity respected; in other words, work with them to establish a reasonable school-night bedtime and be flexible when it comes to determining weekend times for lights out.

Car Trips

A peaceful car trip, especially a long one, requires preparation. Because children cannot sit still very long in one spot, time your rest stops according to the needs of your particular children for stretching, running, and going to the bathroom, and announce them in advance. The stops should anticipate upcoming trouble and be frequent enough to release tension for the most highly active child in the bunch. Children also crave stimulation, and even if the kind of roadside scenery that excites adults excited them (which it does not), they might not be able to see it from their low perch. Pack toys, games, books, and crayons in a shopping bag for each young child in addition to your emergency supplies of drinks and snacks. Play car games. (How many blue cars, license plates from out of state, fast-food outlets, for example, can you find?) Some parents save a special surprise gift for a particularly tedious part of the trip. Car games are very popular among three to six year olds and some families sing songs together to pass the time. On vacations, older kids may drive you crazy with requests for souvenirs and quarters for rest-stop arcade games. Because the vacation is theirs as well as yours, work within your budget to allow older kids to handle their own spending money. A roll of quarters could last a week if your child is keeping tabs on her own spending. If she is saving some of her *own* money for the next stop, she won't have to wrangle it from you.

For even shorter rides, establish the rules of the road before you set off. Wearing seat belts, for instance, is a non-negotiable issue. If choice of seats is going to be an explosive problem, settle it *before* anyone gets into the car. Children are very territorial, and having to unseat a child at the beginning of a trip is guaranteed to poison the atmosphere. You may decide to flip a coin for the desirable window seats or to rotate seating arrangements at rest stops.

As with seat belt use, children need to understand the dangerous consequences of rowdy behavior. Rather than try to argue with a child who is sitting in the backseat (dangerous in itself), you can make your point more forcefully by pulling over to the side of the road and waiting until everyone is quiet again.

Rewarding good behavior with praise or even a small treat ensures an even better trip next time. ("You kids have been so good in the car, we got here early, so we'll have time for a swim before dinner.")

Clothes

Battles about clothing are fought on two fronts: the time it takes to get dressed and the choice of wardrobe. Although most children can dress themselves by the age of five (except to tie their shoes), they often are easily distracted from the task. Parents can help by selecting the clothes with them the night before and then, when they wake up, coming in to see how it's going every few minutes as they get dressed. For kids who are still learning the fine points of self-dressing, look for pants and skirts with elastic waists and shirts that pull over the head, because young children have trouble with buttons and zippers. Be aware, of course, of your child's particular sensibilities; some kids, for example, find *anything* with elastic very uncomfortable. If you still find yourself rushing your child every morning, you just may not be alloting enough time. With older children, always work backward. First decide together how much time they need to get dressed, and then figure out when they have to get up.

Many children—of all ages—have definite and rigid ideas about what clothes they want to wear. If your child says she only likes green sweatpants, you are much wiser to invest in several pairs than to buy neat jeans she will refuse to wear. Most children are happier to get dressed if they helped to select their clothes. When you shop, don't give them a blank check, but let them choose between several outfits that are acceptable to you in price and style.

For some adult events, you may want your children to dress up. Prepare them in advance by explaining the special nature of the occasion and still try to offer several choices. For their own events, your children are more likely than you to know what is de rigueur. Try to grin and bear it.

Teens often assert their independence by choosing outfits that their parents find inappropriate or downright offensive. When they're spending their own money on outrageous fashions, it's even more difficult to influence them. So it's important to choose your battles carefully. Remember to communicate discipline with I-statements and to be empathetic to the needs of teens to fit in with their peers.

Eating

There is no way for parents to control children's appetites, which may change daily or monthly. Some children are finicky eaters by nature, and some children are not hungry at adult mealtimes. Experts consistently advise parents not to become nutrition warriors. Making the dinner table a battleground can lead to eating disorders in the future and upset stomachs right now. If your four year old wants peanut butter every day for lunch, let her have it. Preschoolers and grade-schoolers are notorious for developing food jags. If they are hungry off-schedule, have nutritious snacks available for those times. Your pediatrician should be the judge of whether your children are growing properly, in spite of what they are or are not eating.

There are some ways, however, to make meals more appealing to children. Many children like to participate in preparing the meal—choosing the menu, cooking, and setting the table. Having chosen string beans over spinach for the dinner vegetable and then having helped you slice them, a child is much more likely to eat them. Children like food that is served attractively (to them): peach halves with raisin eyes or a slice of turkey with the child's name printed on it in catsup. Children will also follow your lead and are much more likely to savor healthy foods and balanced meals if you do.

Family meals are much more pleasant if the focus is on conversation and sharing the day's events rather than on a list of complaints or on the food that remains on the child's plate. It helps to remember that when a child leaves food on her plate, it's a sure sign that she's had enough to eat. Try, too, to be relaxed about table manners at home. Children can understand that they have to be more polite in public—when they are visiting or at a restaurant—if they are prepared in advance. Because young children cannot sit still very long, excuse them from the table as soon as they are finished.

Homework

In its brochure, the Town School in New York City describes an ideal for homework:

> Homework is a contract between a child and a teacher. Parents are encouraged to talk with their children about their work and to provide an atmosphere that is conducive to studying. The purpose of homework is to develop a child's study skills and ability to do independent work, to reinforce what has been taught in class, and to extend learning. If a child cannot manage homework alone, it is important to communicate that to the teacher.

Ideally, then, the parents' main role is to help their children set the best time and place to do their homework. Some children like to get homework over with right after school so that the evening will be free. Some children need a snack and some physical exercise before they can settle down to work. Some children need isolation and quiet in order to concentrate, some like to work where others are working or be near an adult. Parents should insist on a regular homework plan, but children should have a say in what it will be. Once it is established, however, there should be no need for nagging, pleading, negotiating, or threatening.

After that, the parents' role is to be a resource: to be available, not hovering, to answer questions without doing the work themselves; to be interested, but not overly critical. (One grade—from the teacher—is all any child needs.) Parents who do their children's homework for them give them the message that they are not capable of doing it themselves.

If homework becomes a problem, parents should contact the teacher to find out what exactly is expected of them and of the child.

"I Want!"

"I want . . . I want . . . I want . . ." is a familiar chorus in most families. It is normal and healthy for a child to want things. In fact, it is a sign of curiosity about the world, a trait that parents should encourage. But every child also needs to learn reasonable limits, and every parent has to decide what these are.

Children who receive plenty of love and attention from their parents usually can accept the limits, if they are clearly stated and consistently applied. This means when your child says, "I want . . ." something you cannot afford or don't want your child to have you say no, not maybe. And when she starts whining, you still say, no, not, "Oh, all right." Parents might explain to their children that in their family gifts are for special occasions, such as holidays and birthdays, or as thank-you's for being a good sport— waiting patiently while Mom does her banking, for instance. Children yearning for love and attention, on the other hand, will not be satisfied by even a shipload of toys and candy.

One mother of a five year old thought up a unique solution to the "I want!" problem. She labeled a large manila envelope "Sascha Wants," and whenever Sascha asked for something, she told him to cut out the picture from the magazine where he saw it, draw a picture of it himself, or write its name on a slip of paper. He then put these in his envelope to save for a gift-giving occasion. Before each of these occasions, she'd ask him to look through the envelope and pick out what he wanted from her and others. To both their surprise, he often ended up discarding much of the contents of his envelope. Besides solving her immediate problem of a child nagging for toys, this mother was also taking her child seriously, while teaching him to be discriminating and to delay gratification.

Room Cleaning

There are three possible solutions to the messy-room problem: Clean it up yourself, make your child clean it up, or ignore it. Most parents are unwilling to do the first. Many experts recommend the second and offer some helpful approaches. But according to the newsletter of the Parents League of New York, at a workshop of 60 parents, "it was almost unanimously agreed that the best solution is to 'close the door' and to stop trying to coerce a youngster into cleaning up. As one mother said, 'When they run out of clean clothes, or when something they really want to wear isn't in wearable condition, they start to get the message.' ''

The acceptability of following this hands-off policy depends on the nature of both the child and the parent. For parents who are messy themselves and thus have weak grounds for enforcing neatness in their children, it may be the best solution. But parents should also know their child well enough to know if she actually *wants* an enforced cleanup. Some children will welcome the push to get their lives in order.

Parents who want to teach their child to be neat should try to do so while still respecting the privacy of their child's room. Explain that although the room belongs to the child, it is also part of a house with certain standards of neatness. State your expectations, which should not be overly demanding, and provide details. The vague instruction to "Clean up your room" may have a very different meaning to the child than to the parent. You may want the bed made, for instance, and toys and games with small pieces put away by the end of the day.

Then make this possible for the child to accomplish. Provide storage space that is easy to reach and teach young children how and where to put things away. With children who are overwhelmed by the task, some parents set a timer for five or 10 minutes, and after it goes off, help the child finish the job. Set a regular cleanup time, preferably not just before bedtime, when both child and parent may be too testy to do it without a fight.

Shopping

Most shopping trips are for the benefit of parents, not children. To ensure success, they need to be well planned. Do not set out if your child is tired or hungry, and at the first sign that she is fading, pay and leave, even if you have not finished. You will both survive a dinner without baked potatoes much better than a kicking, screaming tantrum in the middle of a grocery store. Shop, if possible, when stores are least crowded, and prepare a list of exactly what you want.

Successful shopping trips also usually incorporate some reward for the child. For some children the thrill of riding in the seat of the grocery cart is enough reward. Others like to "help" by pushing the cart, searching for items on the shopping list, or putting cans in the cart. Most children also like to be consulted on choices. ("Which kinds of soup should we get this time?" "Does this cereal look good to you? Should we try it for a change?") Be sure to limit the choices, however, to acceptable items.

On some shopping trips (for adult clothes or hardware, for example), there may be no way for the child to participate. Some parents bring along a favorite toy or book or surprise their child with something new and entertaining—an activity book or some plastic figures. At the grocery store, too, a mother might promise her child one purchase of her own or a ride on the toy spaceship outside as a reward for her patience. In any case, a young child who behaves well on a grown-up shopping trip deserves praise.

Television

There are conflicting opinions about the exact effects of television on children. Some maintain that it is educational; others insist that it's mind numbing and violence inducing. There is no question, however, of television's seductive power for children. There is also no question that it is a standard feature in most homes.

Although it would be hard for television-watching parents to deny television to their children entirely, you can still teach them to use the television in moderation. Some parents limit the time their children watch to a certain number of hours a day or to just the weekends. They may also monitor and comment on the shows the children choose (including the commercials).

Other parents treat watching television as an event, like going to the movies. They allow their children to watch special shows, chosen in advance from reviews or recommendations. The television is turned on at the beginning of the show and turned off at the end. This discourages the habit some children (and adults) have of automatically turning on the television and flipping channels in search of anything that catches their eye.

Once these rules are set, however, parents have to be careful not to cheat and use the television as a baby-sitter whenever they are busy. Parents also should appreciate the great influence their own television-watching habits will have on their children. If you come home from work and immediately plop yourself in front of the television, how can you expect your children to come home from school and do otherwise?

CHAPTER SIX

••••••

Dealing with Unacceptable Behavior

O. Henry's story *The Ransom of Red Chief* is about a little boy who was so badly behaved that when he was kidnapped his abductors ended up paying his parents to take him back. This story brings a wry smile to the faces of most parents—not because their children are monsters, but because every kid does a few things that are just awful. This chapter is dedicated to addressing those behaviors that you just can't tolerate. (One exception is tantrums. Because they are so common in toddlers and preschoolers, we have discussed them as a developmental issue in chapter 2.)

Probably the single biggest key to dealing with unacceptable behavior is to define exactly what unacceptable behavior is. If you narrowly define what you consider to be unacceptable, it will be much easier for you and your child to understand that certain issues are absolutely nonnegotiable. When a transgression occurs and you find it necessary to apply a punishment, your punishments will make a big impression—not because the punishment is severe, but because it is seldom invoked.

Your decision about what is acceptable will be in some ways unique to you and your child. Some parents may find raucous behavior in the house—wrestling or shouting and jostling—intolerable. Other parents may not mind it as much. Different parents will tolerate differing degrees of of the same behavior. For instance, in some families, swearing is considered a serious offense; in others, swearing is just another way of expressing oneself.

Defining the Problem

Dr. Stanley Turecki, who has done research on the problems of children who are temperamentally difficult, has devised some guidelines for parents of such children. In his book *The Difficult Child* (coauthored with Leslie Tonner) Dr. Turecki states that parents of difficult children often fall into frustrating and futile patterns of reaction, nagging, and punishment, so it is especially important for them to pick and choose their issues with care. Dr. Turecki suggests that parents ask the following thoughtful questions that cut to the heart of the matter:

1. **Is this important?** How much does this behavior affect your own and the child's life? Issues such as a toddler's throwing things in the house, which irritate you, may not be as crucial as aggressiveness, which impairs your child's relationship with his age-mates. For older children, issues such as cleaning their rooms may not be as serious as not doing their homework. Is the issue something that irritates you so much that it is *affecting the overall quality of your relationship with your child*? One example might be extreme irresponsibility for chores and possessions: habitually leaving the care of a pet up to you or repeatedly losing or damaging things because they are left outside overnight.
2. **To what degree is the behavior a problem?** To cite the

example of irresponsibility: Does your child leave his bike on the front lawn whenever he isn't using it? Does he constantly dump his sneakers, baseball glove, and jacket wherever he happens to be at the moment and leave them there? Does he always lose library books, homework assignments, and other important things? Does he do one of the above, or all three? Does he do this every day, or once every couple of weeks?

3. **Do both parents agree that the issue is important?** Because consistency is a must for getting across the seriousness of these issues, parents should come to a consensus.

   It is very interesting to note that in Drs. Chess and Thomas' "New York Longitudinal Study" (more fully discussed in chapter 2), the only one of a number of parental "mistakes" that they found to be really detrimental to children's progress was *serious* disagreements between parents about how children should be raised.

4. **Are you being objective?** It can be terribly difficult to be objective about your child's worst behavior. Step back and try to see the problem through two other people's eyes, for example, your child's or your spouse's. Ask yourself if you are being *fair*. Expectations can be unfair when you ask a child to behave in a way that he is not developmentally ready or temperamentally fit for, or when you ask things of a child that you wouldn't ask of yourself or perhaps of another child. Unfairness leads to battles of will. Battles of will can lead to harsh or frequent punishments and intense arguments. These, in turn, can lead to hostility and defiance.

   An example of an expectation that is not a good fit with developmental readiness might be expecting a preschooler to get dressed by himself by a certain time. Mastery over the skills connected with self-dressing come to different children at different times; a child may have some skills but not others. Some children may need more supervision; others benefit from having their clothes laid out in the order in which they'll be put on. Most young children have only a vague sense of time; if time is of the essence, put a kitchen timer where the child can see it, challenge the child to a race, or change the morning routine so that the child gets up earlier or has fewer tasks to complete.

As illustrated in chapter 2, temperament can be at the heart of some discipline battles. For instance, a child whose system is rather irregular won't be able to settle down for bed at the same time every night. Deciding on a "lights out" hour and sticking to it with this child is setting the stage for war. In this case, it is reasonable to insist on a bedtime, at which time the child must stay in his room or in his bed, reading or playing quietly.

Other temperamental attributes that, when misunderstood, commonly lead to "discipline" problems are low distractibility (you can't get your child to stop doing what he's doing and come when he's called); low sensory threshold (the child will tolerate only certain clothes, foods, etc.); and short attention span (he forgets tasks or gets sidetracked in the middle of tasks). In each case, the appropriate way to change the behavior is to work *with* the temperament, *not against* it. Give stubborn children warnings ("In five minutes, we are going to the store"), and give them time to settle down a bit between activities. Let sensitive children guide your choices when it comes to their clothes and food and environment. Give children with short attention spans appropriate tasks that are quick to accomplish. Remind them when it is time to do a chore.

Some children with short attention spans respond well to having a calendar on which their responsibilities are spelled out: 6:30 p.m., Monday, Wednesday, and Friday—take out the garbage.

You may be surprised to find that there are behaviors that you expect from your child that you don't expect from yourself. One of the behaviors that most irritates parents is one that they often do to their children: interrupting. How often do you answer the phone on the first ring while your child is talking to you or while the two of you are engaged in some other activity? Do you habitually respond to an adult speaking to you even if you are talking with your child, effectively pushing the child aside to pay attention to the adult? Again, the best way to teach your children to behave with respect is to treat them with respect.

Expecting from one child what you don't expect from another is also a common pitfall. Sometimes this is justified in the name of each child's individual personality and needs, but sometimes it reflects deeply rooted sexual stereotypes. (A boy might be expected to do yard work that his sister isn't counted on to handle, or his sister might be required to make beds, a task which the boy is allowed to neglect.) Sometimes it is worthwhile to deny one child something minor for the sake of fairness and consistency. The parents of Mark, age 11, made a rule that there would be no television before dinner so that Mark could concentrate on his homework. This meant that his four-year-old brother, Rick, did not get to watch his favorite shows either. Rick did okay without television, and instead used the time to ''help'' his parents prepare supper, and the firmness of the rule made it much easier for Mark to abide by it.

If you feel satisfied that the behaviors you find unacceptable are truly unacceptable, if both parents are in agreement about them, and if you believe that your expectations are fair, then it is time to take action.

Dangerous and/or Wrong Behaviors

Most parents find that after they've asked themselves these questions, the behaviors that stand out as really unacceptable are those that are physically dangerous, morally wrong, or both.

There are some subtle differences in how we should best deal with dangerous behaviors and those that are morally wrong. For instance, *you* can cross the street by yourself, but your preschooler or toddler cannot. Getting ideas of safety across often involves the child's doing what you say, not what you do. (Your child's actual observations—that everyone else seems to cross streets just fine—quite naturally make your rules seem ridiculous.) You need to protect him from risks until he has the maturity to make good judgments himself.

In the case of behaviors that are dangerous because children do not understand the risks—playing in the street, crossing the street without permission, and throwing things—it is important that your response be *immediate*. Not only do you want to protect your child, but you want to show that this cannot be tolerated for even a minute.

In such a situation, because the child cannot really understand why what he has done is unacceptable, punishment can only seem unfair and overpowering to the child. It may even prompt defiance and encourage him to repeat the action.

Time-out, on the other hand, is quite effective for misbehaviors involving safety issues, especially for younger children. Time-out works in part because the boredom of it lands on kids pretty heavily. Therefore, make sure that your time-out locale is appropriate for the age of your child (where he can be supervised if the child is very young; where he will have no toys, no window, no oblique glimpse of the television if he is older).

You must tell the child why he has to have this time-out. *Be brief:* "You have to have time-out because you are not allowed to cross the street by yourself." Do not nag or lecture, do not obscure your message in an avalanche of words and rhetorical questions. Do not repeat yourself. The quickest way to condition your child to stop listening to you is to repeat orders, instructions, and rules.

A variation of time-out is to prevent a child from returning to the "scene of the crime" for an appropriate length of time. For example, Toby refused to obey her mother and stop arguing with her little brother in the car. As a result, she was not allowed to go out with the family in the car for three days. When Louanne pushed an empty swing at the park too hard, and it almost hit another child in the face, Louanne was not allowed to go back to the park for the rest of the week.

The same principle can be applied to bicycles, toys, and other possessions, when the issue is taking responsibility for one's things. Lynn Clark, author of *The Time-Out Solution*, suggests using time-out with a toy when it is an accessory to misbehavior. ("You left your bike in the driveway again, so you can't use it for three days.")

As children get older, time-out becomes harder to apply and is less effective because older children can amuse themselves with their thoughts—such as how to get back at you or how to get away with the misbehavior the next time. Therefore, grounding is more appropriate for children at the older end of the school-age spectrum, because it combines the removal from the scene offered by the time-out solution with a revocation of privileges.

For preteen children, certain privileges signify independence and growing up to them. If a misbehavior is really serious, withdrawing privileges is a meaningful punishment. This works best when the privileges revoked are connected to the misbehavior. For example, Nathalie and her friends went downtown without permission one day, something she was absolutely not allowed to do. Her mother didn't know where she was, which frightened her enough, but she also knew that at 12 years old, Nathalie was not old enough to look out for herself in many parts of the city for any length of time.

When Nathalie came home, her mother told her that she was grounded for two weeks and that she would not be allowed to go downtown under any circumstances for a month. The punishment was appropriate to the transgression.

Eleven-year-old Daniel decided to make popcorn when his mother went out to pick up his sister from her ballet class. He was often allowed to cook with his mother, but he knew that one of the ground rules for being allowed to stay alone without a baby-sitter was no cooking, although he couldn't entirely conceptualize the risks. After this episode, Daniel had to suffer the embarrassment of accompanying his mother on short outings or staying with a sitter. Daniel's mother was not punishing Daniel. Strictly speaking, she was showing him, in no uncertain terms, that she had found his behavior unacceptable.

Another way of dealing with unacceptable behavior that is not related to a safety issue is to let children experience the logical consequences of their behavior. For instance, Jonathan continuously neglected to pick up his dirty clothes and put them in the hamper; in response, his mother let the clothes sit there, and eventually his Little League uniform was not clean and ready when he needed it. His punishment—having to wear his messy uniform and having to deal with his coach's and his team's reaction—was a logical outcome of his behavior. If, however, Jonathan's mother had decided that, as punishment for not picking up his clothes, he could not go to the next Little League game, that punishment would have be illogical—i.e., not arising directly from the boy's behavior but from his mother's anger. He would then have seen *her* as the transgressor rather than himself.

When Your Child's Behavior Is Wrong

Just as children may do something that is dangerous without really understanding why, they may also do something morally wrong without understanding *why* it is wrong. Two of the most common childhood "sins" come under this rubric: lying and stealing.

For little children, the world is more or less an oyster always holding out the tantalizing possibility of a pearl. It never occurs to them that the pearl doesn't automatically belong to them. All toys have the potential of being *their* toys.

Stealing in quite young children is not stealing as we know it. There is no malice or notion of wrongdoing; children will just pick things up because they look pretty. But you must tell them that it is *never* okay to take something without paying for it and show them how to return it. You can say, "Taking something without paying for it is against the law." Children take laws and authority very seriously. Because of this, it is best to be careful about accusing or labeling children ("You are stealing!" "You're a liar!").

These words carry enormous social baggage that can cause children to feel extreme and unwarranted guilt.

By the same token, words and actions can have blurry boundaries. When a three or four year old who has been playing ball in the living room tells you that it wasn't he who broke a lamp, he may not really understand that *saying* so doesn't *make* it so.

It is very important when confronting issues of tale-telling that *you* make things clear for the child. Do not ask, "Did you break the lamp?" when you know very well that he did. Tell him you know that he broke the lamp and apply whatever consequences you have decided are merited for throwing balls in the house. Always point out the difference between fantasy and reality to small children ("You wish you didn't break the lamp, but the lamp is broken. That is what happens when you play ball in the house"). When an older child lies, you must point out the wrongness of lying as well ("You get 10 minutes time-out for playing ball in the house and then another 20 minutes for not being honest with me about it"). Children can understand the importance of saying "I'm sorry," but reparations should also be made. Older children may be able to pay for damage caused, but all children can give extra time in chores as part payment for something they have broken. The idea of being able to take part in making something right is very healing. Everyone feels better.

If lying or stealing persists, especially in older children, there may be a deeper problem. It does not help to attack further such a child's self-esteem by using labels, but as part of getting to the problem, he should deal with the consequences of returning stolen items himself and being confronted with lies.

Unlike safety issues, in which you ask the child to do as you say and not as you do, when dealing with issues of morality, you ask that the child do as you say *and* do. You, for example, cannot hit other adults with impunity any more than your child can hit his playmates. Getting ideas of morality across involves modeling behavior, teaching empathy, and helping your child learn positive ways to express anger or other feelings.

Sometimes a behavior requires a combination of approaches: If your preschooler is throwing his blocks at his friends, he probably does not and cannot understand how badly he might hurt the other children. His sense of right and wrong is undeveloped, so he needs to learn to think empathically, to be directed into other modes of emotional expression, and to reflect on the fact that when Mommy and Daddy are upset, they don't throw things.

There are times when your child *knows* that something he is doing is wrong, *understands why* it is wrong, and does it anyway. This is not an indication that he's headed for a life of crime. When a child willfully defies your standards, it's important to look at *why* he's doing so. Does he crave your attention? Negative attention is, after all, better than no attention at all from you. Is he trying to get revenge for something he judges you to have done wrong? Is he upset by something going on at home, at school, or with his friends? When dealing with the unacceptable behavior, be sure to separate the behavior from the child. (The behavior is bad; he is not.) Be sure, too, that the punishment is appropriate. Overreacting and punishing too severely will most likely increase the defiance. Be firm *and* fair.

When Others Are Involved

Teasing and tattling are two of the more unpleasant forms of social misbehavior that older kids invariably try out. Time-out a teaser and tune out a tattler; both methods take the perpetrator away from his intended audience. For the same reason, tuning out is also the right approach to whining. (The point should be made, however, that tattling does not mean not telling parents something important—as in cases where someone could get hurt if the child *doesn't* tell. Kids should be encouraged to tell parents if a sibling or a friend is in trouble.)

Teasing and tattling often involve peer pressure—the motive behind many unacceptable behaviors. Here again, empathy is invaluable in helping a child to react as an individual toward other individuals, not as a member of a pack. Try role-playing dialogue in which your child is the one who is excluded—or the one who stands up for what is right. Young children will typically pick up copycat behaviors such as swearing or spitting. Making an absurd game out of copying can drive a point home. With older children, however, peer pressure is more subtle and requires a more thoughtful response.

You show how much you respect individual moral judgment in two ways: by expressing clear disapproval for bad choices and by modeling good choices. Moral values are not responsive to a carrot-and-stick approach. If you punish too severely, your child learns the moral of deviousness and avoidance. If you go overboard with rewards, he never learns to do the good thing for its own sake.

As children near adolescence, the drive to be independent of their parents as well as the drive to conform with their age-mates is very strong. At this age, children respond very negatively to coercive discipline. Pointing out that everyone *always* has a choice whether to do right or wrong— and helping children learn to come up with their own choices—is probably the most productive thing you can do. A person who feels he has a choice is not a blind follower.

The Goals of Misbehavior

Don Dinkmeyer and Gary D. McKay, authors of the *STEP* handbook, believe that children seek to achieve certain goals through bad behavior. One of the commonest goals, the easiest to recognize and do something about, is that of gaining attention. If you tell a three year old to stop screeching and he screeches louder, this is probably his aim. A nine year old who deliberately flouts an after-school curfew may be sending you the same signal.

Another, unfortunately common, goal of bad behavior is that of exercising power. Children often feel powerless; there are many things they cannot have or do merely because they are children. Occasionally parents exacerbate a child's need for power by using certain overpowering forms of discipline. If you notice that your child seems to need revenge when you have disciplined him, ask yourself if the forms of discipline you are using are appropriate to your child's age, temperament, and behavior. For example, putting a four year old in time-out for an hour would be overkill, no matter how serious the offense was. The child would be overwhelmed by his situation because he can't handle so much time in isolation. For older children, any form of discipline that humiliates the child in front of his peers is also likely to cause very destructive feelings.

If you are caught in a power dynamic with a child, the best thing you can to is to depersonalize it. Concentrate on the behavior and not on the child—or on yourself. Good communication can help children learn to handle the frustrations and limitations inherent in being young. Stick to applying reasonable and logical consequences, and try to communicate without accusing. Saying ''This room needs to be cleaned,'' is much less likely to push the power button than ''I told you to do it yesterday.''

The most upsetting goal of bad behavior is what the *STEP* handbook terms a ''display of inadequacy.'' Sometimes when a child is really discouraged, he behaves the way he thinks a bad and worthless child is expected to behave. If things have gotten out of hand and you suspect that your child's troublemaking stems from this sort of despair, the only solution is to react as little and as neutrally as possible to bad behavior and to respond to any positive behavior very enthusiastically.

This does not mean suspending all limits, but it means enforcing limits calmly and lovingly. It means spending time with this child, listening to him, and letting him know, often, that you love him. Your child needs to know that there is a marked difference between how you view him and how you view his behavior. Although you may not love what he does, he must be assured that you love who he is.

What About Spanking?

Spanking is the word we use to describe hitting someone smaller than ourselves. Parents often use innocuous words such as *smack, bop,* or *potchky* to refer to physical punishment. These words take the sting out of what we're doing. Does sparing the rod spoil the child? Yes. But it's important to realize that the ''rod'' is a shepherd's staff, used to *guide* wandering sheep, not a stick used to beat them. While a single incidence of hitting a child does not establish child abuse, a pattern of hitting them can constitute abuse. Parents who spank *do* find that their actions have an immediate effect. But effective discipline is not a matter of immediacy. Its goals are long term, and spanking has no long-term benefits. Its long-term effects are, in fact, counterproductive. It's difficult to teach a child that his body belongs to him and that he should respect himself when those who love him most violate his physical boundaries and inflict pain.

According to a number of surveys, parents who have spanked their children in the past and who have stopped, say that they gave it up because it became necessary to hit their children harder and harder each time.

Daria, the mother of nine-year-old Peter and seven-year-old Mark, for example, gave up spanking when her youngest was no longer a toddler. "I don't think that a quick thwack on the bottom when a kid does something particularly annoying or dangerous is child abuse," she says. "But I could see that as Pete was getting bigger and more independent he was testing me more, and I would get angrier. I realized that if I was relying on spanking to make him understand when I thought something was really bad, the day was going to come when I would have to wallop him."

Many parents are also disturbed by the double message physical punishment carries: How can we teach a child self-respect and respect for the rights and property of others when we use a method that so offends the child's dignity? Effective discipline techniques are fair, consistent, and direct children toward behaviors we'd like them to exhibit on a permanent basis. Spanking just doesn't fit this bill.

CHAPTER SEVEN

· · · · · ·

Dealing with Anger— Yours and Your Kids'

When I was little I never talked back to my parents. If I was angry at them, I went into my room and sulked, or I beat up my little sister, but I never, *never* talked back to them," one mother recalls. "Now when my son Jason gets mad at me, I don't know what to do. I don't want to squash him and say, 'Don't talk to me like that.' On the other hand, it upsets me and embarrasses me— especially when there are other people around."

Dealing with anger is one of the hardest jobs parents have. "Our society has a taboo on anger for both adults *and* children," says Dr. Henry Paul, a child psychiatrist and faculty member of the department of psychiatry at the Columbia College of Physicians and Surgeons and at Mt. Sinai Medical Center in New York City and an expert on children's anger. "Children are supposed to be nice and polite, especially to grown-ups. But that doesn't work all the time. Telling a child she *can't* get angry is like saying she can't breathe, she can't love."

When Kids Get Angry

When a child is not permitted to express anger it stays inside, and buried anger can turn into feelings of helplessness, isolation, and rage.

In *The Angry Book,* New York City psychiatrist and writer, Dr. Theodore Isaac Rubin describes healthy anger in the following ways:

It's intense. Blood may rush to the child's face. She may yell and use strong language. But that is not a sign of disrespect; strong language is more fittingly seen as "the poetry of anger."

It's direct. Parent and child talk to each other with lots of feeling, and they stay put. Nobody runs away.

It's immediate. It happens right away, and it's short-lived. It quickly burns itself out.

It brings tensions out and can help to ease them. Often, parent and child feel better after the feelings have been expressed.

Helping Kids Deal with Their Anger

Is it dangerous to let children express their anger? Doesn't it make them violent and disrespectful?

No, says Dr. Paul. Anger is a natural process, like eating or loving, but many parents have been so "well brought up" that they have trouble tolerating it. The important thing, he stresses, is *how* the anger is expressed. Parents should set clear and definite limits concerning this. "Violence is *not* acceptable. Tantrums in the supermarket are *not* acceptable," Dr. Paul stresses. But as long as their child's anger is not overly aggressive or violent, parents should accept it, because healthy anger is an important form of communication for children as well as adults.

When a child is angry, parents need to be open, responsive, and sympathetic. Cold words won't do. Dr. Rubin cites a mother whose child was throwing sand at the playground. The mother called her son over and gave him a lecture on playground ethics. Then, without any feeling, she said, "I am angry." It didn't mean a thing to the child, Dr. Rubin claims, because "no contact had been made."

Both Dr. Rubin and Dr. Paul suggest that parents react with feeling. ("I *know* you're angry, but I can't let you hit me. I *have* to go to work, but I'll be back at dinnertime.")

Sometimes, they agree, a child's anger should be ignored (such as during an attention-getting tantrum at home). Other times, it should be confronted ("Tell me why you are yelling; help me understand what's bothering you"). Each situation has to be evaluated on its individual merits and according to the needs of each child.

After the storm is over, parents should look at what caused it. Sometimes a child's anger comes from the ordinary difficulties of growing up, but other times it's a danger sign, a red flag hoisted by the child, saying, "Help me! I'm in trouble."

What Makes Children Angry?

Lots of different things make children angry. Some of the most common causes of children's anger include:

The simple frustrations of being a child. Example, Charlie, age two, wants the colored pencils. He strains toward them, his fingers wiggling, his face red. Seeing that he can't quite reach them, his father comes over and hands them to him. That *really* makes Charlie mad. He bursts into tears. "This kind of frustration is a fact of life," says Dr. Paul. "Parents need to be sympathetic and patient. In the end, children learn the skills they need."

Separations. For example, three-year-old Sandra doesn't want her mother to go to work, so she lines up her stuffed animals in front of the door. When her mother tries to move them, Sandra sobs wildly. It looks like unhappiness, but Sandra's reaction can just as well be anger. Separations bring out a variety of difficult feelings in children.

"Separations are very hard for young children, but it doesn't help for a mother to give in to her child's dramatic behavior," Dr. Paul asserts. "She needs to reassure her child and say that she'll be back. After a while, when the child sees her mother disappearing and reappearing, she'll learn that although separation is painful it is not life threatening."

Rules and regulations. For example, Randy, nine years old, is convinced that it would be exciting to ride her bicycle across a busy intersection. When her father says it is dangerous, she doesn't believe him. When he makes her walk across the street, she is furious.

Randy's father wants to save her from an accident. He also wants to help her develop more realistic ideas about what she can do. Her anger is understandable, but her father's actions are totally appropriate. Children's feelings don't disappear just because their parents are acting in the name of reason.

"Children often overrate their abilities. They don't have an accurate idea of what they can do. For safety's sake, they have to be limited," Dr. Paul advises. However, these limitations can seem unfair, and children may react with anger.

School problems. When a child comes home from school feeling angry, it isn't always easy to tell what's wrong. Parents need to investigate. Talk to the child, preferably during a quiet time later. Ask questions in a nonaccusatory way.

"Sometimes the problem is a tough teacher, in which case the parent needs to go to school and see what can be done," says Dr. Paul. "Or sometimes it's a perceptual problem." The child may be falling behind in her schoolwork because she can't see the blackboard. Or, another student could be creating tension in her. Parents have to find out the source of their child's anger.

The wrong kind of care. For example, one-year-old Jesse turns red and screams whenever his mother tries to diaper him. "Who could believe that a young baby could get so mad?" she says. "But I know an angry face when I see one."

One day a friend asks her if she is diapering her son too often. Says Jesse's mother, "I realized I was trying to prove I was a perfect mother—I changed his diapers so much he got to hate it." Since then she has cut down and given Jesse some peace and finds that he gets angry less often.

Another example is Carl who made his small, delicate son, Jack, join an after-school sports club. Every Tuesday and Thursday Jack comes home tired, discouraged, and angry. He finds that he is terrible at sports. Jack tries to make it clear that he would much rather stay home and draw pictures, but Carl is so intent on having an athlete in the family that he doesn't listen. He forces Jack to stay in the club.

Finding that his anger is not getting the desired results, Jack has to keep it inside. He becomes bitter and withdrawn to the point that his teacher complains he isn't paying attention in school.

Hidden Anger

How can parents tell when their child has a problem with anger? Here are a few situations that indicate possible trouble:

- **Perfect behavior.** Everybody gets angry from time to time. A child who is "perfect" and never gets angry could very well be hiding her feelings, because for some reason she has learned not to express them.

- **Unexpected flare-ups.** When a child gets wildly, unreasonably angry over something small, it's often a sign that there's a backlog of anger.

- **Depression.** A child who can't express her anger may turn it against herself and become depressed. Depression can take many forms, such as overeating, oversleeping, and having problems in school.

- **Inappropriate behavior.** Occasional tantrums are normal for a two year old, but an older child should be able to express anger in a more controlled way. Chronic tantrums are never normal. Violence against people or objects is never acceptable. Parents need to examine why their children express anger in socially unacceptable ways.

It can sometimes be difficult for parents—because they are with their children day in and day out—to judge the difference between angers that are okay and angers that are not. What is "chronic" anger when most kids can get furious at least once a day? Siblings are nearly always wrestling and poking each other; when is it too violent? Toys often get thrown while children are still learning better ways to express rage; when is it destructive?

A good rule of thumb is that there is a problem when angers affect the child's life in general. If other children shy away from your child at school, for example, it may be a sign that she needs help taking care of an anger that's too hot for her to handle.

"I never really understood that Brian's being angry so often was a deeper problem until his nursery school teacher brought it to my attention," says Linda, a journalist. "The teacher told me that he was too aggressive and alienated a lot of the other kids. She was worried that if this continued and he got used to seeing himself that way, once he started school, things would get worse. I realized it was time for Brian to get some real therapy. After a short time the therapist helped me see that I had been expecting too much from Brian, expecting him to act like a six year old even though he was only four. Once I let up on him at home, his behavior at school improved almost instantly. I'm grateful to that teacher because I just couldn't quite see it."

Healthy anger is direct, uncomplicated, and easy to recognize. Hidden anger has a hundred faces. The important thing for parents to remember is that *any* form of unhappy behavior, from teasing to overeating to inattention in school, can be the result of hidden anger. And Dr. Paul has found that repressed anger is one of the most important causes of emotional problems in children.

Accepting Children's Anger

"I love being a parent, but I *hate* the angry part," Jason's mother says. "When Jason gets angry at me, I feel so uncomfortable and unhappy."

But, Dr. Rubin cautions, one cannot and should not escape anger. "Negate anger and you must also negate love. You simply can't have one feeling without the other. Love, like anger, requires a real self and a real exchange."

For parents who never learned the positive benefits of expressing anger themselves, children provide a second chance. "Dealing with the raw emotions of children can often be very healing for parents," notes Dr. Paul, "if the parents are open enough."

When Parents Get Angry

"When Zack was little, it seemed as if I was angry at him half the time," one mother remembers. "He was terribly messy. He wouldn't use a spoon. There'd be a ring of food around his chair. I'd have to wash him and the floor after every meal."

Sometimes his mother felt very guilty about getting angry at Zack; after all, he was only a little child. Other times she found herself a little frightened by her strong feelings. "I was turning into the kind of person I'd never seen myself being—shouting and carrying on." But when she felt angry, her feelings came out; what else could she do?

Everyone Gets Angry

Zack's mother's actions were both common and natural; anger is an unavoidable part of life. "Getting angry, like getting hungry, is a natural human phenomenon, and neither needs an excuse for being," writes Dr. Rubin. "Getting angry is neither right nor wrong. It just is."

Many people have difficulty with the idea that anger is natural. For some, getting angry goes against the image they have of themselves as a "good person, a nice guy." For others, any show of anger is like a loss of control, something that is to be avoided. Learning how to be "healthily angry" is difficult for anyone, Dr. Rubin admits, but it is possible.

Expressing anger in a healthy, productive way is hard enough when an adult is the target. But when an adult's anger is aimed at a child, it becomes a much more complicated problem. Children are vulnerable and do not have the emotional resources or experience that adults have for dealing with anger. And yet, parents naturally find that many things their children do anger them, most obviously, when a child disobeys. The parent will feel angry, resentful, and may even "lose her cool." These strong feelings bring up big questions: "Is it proper for me to get angry at my child?" "How can I express my anger?" "When is my anger too much?"

Such big questions are often difficult for parents, many of whom are hesitant to talk about their anger. Some are afraid to admit their feelings, fearing the disapproval of others. "There's a cultural taboo about parents getting mad," says R. Thomas Lopez, a child psychoanalyst at the Center for Preventive Psychiatry in White Plains, New York. "If you get angry, it's not that it's a hard world, it's that you're a bad parent. Very often, parents are enormously guilt ridden about reacting normally to life.''

Allowing Anger

Anger is a normal response to irritating things. However, there are many ways of expressing anger. Immediate anger is very different from unconscious, suppressed anger. With immediate anger, the parent is expressing what she feels about what is happening at the moment. For example, a typical power struggle with a child may end with the parent saying, ''I've tried and tried to be fair with you, Bobby, but you keep disobeying me. Now I'm furious!'' The parent is angry and knows why she is angry. Her voice may be raised, she might even restrain or hold her child—but her anger is clearly a reponse to the immediate situation.

The second type of anger takes the parent by surprise. It may be the smallest thing—your daughter asking you a question—that will suddenly set off an explosive expression of anger. Experts believe that this explosive anger often grows out of a failure to express smaller feelings of anger. If small upsets are not expressed, they do not necessarily dissipate, but can be held inside. Finally, they may be released in one big explosion.

Some parents hold back their feelings of anger, believing that any expression of anger is bad for their children. But Dr. Lopez points out that this can be counterproductive. Suppressing anger not only buries feelings that may surface later but also confuses the child. ''Coldness and formality are signs of hidden anger,'' she says, signs that the child will pick up as surely as he picks up anger directly expressed. If parents are angry, they should allow themselves to let their feelings out. In short, Dr. Lopez says, ''they can act like people.'' Not to do so—to withdraw or withhold affection from the child or to ignore her—may be much more destructive than expressing anger would be, he adds.

Keeping Your Cool

Sometimes your anger at your child may overwhelm you. What, then, can you do to keep your anger from getting out of control? The following are some suggestions for coping with your anger.

Determine the source of your anger. If you feel yourself getting angry at your child for something small, ask yourself if you are really mad at your child or if other outside factors are involved. The stress of a job and the hassles of everyday life can often put people on edge, and a child's normal behavior can trigger anger caused by something else. If you find yourself blowing up at your child for reasons that are not her fault, it's important to let her know the source of your anger and that she's not to blame. Even a young child will be reassured when you say, "I'm angry, but it has nothing to do with you."

Sometimes the source of your anger really doesn't have much to do with your child; you may have been up late finishing your tax returns every night that week, you might be on a crash diet, or perhaps office politics are taking a toll on you. Overtired kids have a hair trigger for anger and so do most overtired and overstressed adults.

Sometimes, too, a parent may suspect that her feelings are out of line. Some angers are personal; if you just feel "upset" or "angry"—as opposed to upset or angry about something—it may help to get professional insight into your feelings. One of the best ways to show children the value you place on honest and appropriate expression of emotions is to let them see you act honestly and display feelings openly.

Keep your sense of humor. Although it may be difficult when you feel angry, maintaining a sense of humor will help you keep the matter in proportion. Dr. Istar Schwager, educational psychologist and research director for *Sesame Street Magazine Parents' Guide*, points out that "it's important for parents to keep a sense of proportion and not to think that a child's inattentiveness or disobedience are signals of terrible things to come ('My child's never going to listen to me if he doesn't listen to me now')."

If you are overwhelmed by your anger, leave the room. Sometimes anger simply explodes. In these cases, if possible, it may be best to get away and express it somewhere else. At the very least, removing yourself can give you some time to calm down. Dr. Schwager cautions parents, however, not to withdraw silently. Tell your child why you're leaving: "I'm very angry now and need some time to calm down. I'll talk to you about this later."

Develop a vocabulary of anger. The language of anger is very important. "Anger shouldn't be expressed in the form of blaming," Dr. Schwager says. Rather than tell your child she's been bad, learn to express your anger in specific ways, through an I-statement such as "It upsets me when you don't listen" or "I'm really in a hurry and it makes me so frustrated when you spend so much time with your toys." (For more on I-statements, see chapter 4, pages 74–75.) Dr. Schwager stresses, "It's really important for parents to be very clear on what their needs are and why. Part of the whole issue of positive expression of anger is that children and adults learn why a person is angry."

Defuse anger before it escalates. Every parent encounters situations that will invariably provoke feelings of anger: the temper tantrum in the supermarket or the clinging when you must leave for work. There are ways, however, to reduce the number of anger-provoking situations you encounter before they become problems. "It's important for parents to work out methods of not letting anger escalate," Dr. Schwager advises. Let your child know what to expect next so that there is more of an understanding and communication of what you need from your child. For example, if your child tends to dawdle, give her a warning that she has a few minutes to clean up her toys, rather than wait until it's too late. Or if your child clings to you and screams each morning when you are about to leave for work, thus making you late, start the day 15 minutes earlier and give her some more attention.

When Is It Too Much?

Getting angry at your child is natural. But sometimes a parent's anger can escalate beyond reason, creating stress in the child and guilt in the parent. "It's important for parents to maintain a sense of control, even when they're angry," says Dr. Schwager, "to realize that even though they may be very angry, they still are role models for their child in finding appropriate ways of expressing anger." How do you know, then, if you have gone too far? Here are some signals to watch for when you are expressing anger at your child.

- **If you start to shriek.** When you get angry, it is not always easy to be aware of how much anger is being expressed. But volume of voice is a good indicator of when you may have gone too far. If you suddenly hear yourself shrieking, stop. Very loud voices can be frightening, particularly to young children, and they may have trouble hearing the message. Give yourself a moment to cool off, then let the child know that you're aware of your lack of control. Be short and to the point and don't overexplain. "I didn't mean to yell so loud. I'm sorry. I hope I didn't frighten you."

- **If your language becomes abusive.** Sometimes anger can be so intense and overwhelming that you say things you don't really mean and later regret. Telling a child such things as "I can't take you anymore," "You're driving me crazy," and "You're a rotten brat," seriously erodes a child's sense of self-esteem, particularly when such statements are made repeatedly. Instead, use an I-statement to focus on the child's behavior that made you upset rather than on the child as a human being ("It makes me so angry when you . . .").

- **If you become overly punitive.** In the heat of anger, parents may be tempted to dole out sweeping punishments, such as "I'm never going to let you watch television again" or "That's the last toy I ever buy you," although they really don't mean to carry out these threats. This kind of lashing out is a parent's way of trying to assert some control and doesn't help the child to learn anything from the situation.

    Similarly, if a parent finds herself hitting her child in anger, it's teaching the child that solving problems through physical force is okay. For a parent who wants a child to learn verbal methods for solving conflicts, hitting a child does not support that message.

- **If your child reacts with stress.** If you notice your child withdrawing from you or acting distraught, you may have expressed more anger than you needed to get your point across. Most children will respond to a parent who speaks firmly and with conviction. Dr. Schwager emphasizes that "parents needn't feel that they have to see their child acting distraught to know that their words have made an impression. Children are very reliant on their parents and really do take what they say quite seriously."

As parents express their anger in a positive way, they help their children learn how to express their anger, too— a highly valuable lesson for life. Children can come to understand that you can be angry at them and still care for them. That's one of the most important lessons that children *and* adults can learn.

CHAPTER EIGHT

● ● ● ● ● ●

When Parents Disagree on Discipline

Differences between parents about how to discipline their children are normal, according to Nancy Samalin, director of Parent Guidance Workshops in New York City as well as the author of *Loving Your Child Is Not Enough.* In fact, she says, for two parents to have exactly the same views about raising children "is almost a miracle." As intimate as they may be, the mother and father who are now attempting to bring up a child of their own were raised in different families by parents who probably treated them in different ways. One family may have been demonstrative, the other restrained; one family may have been very strict about certain behaviors, the other may have been much more relaxed.

Although children can adjust to differences in style, "parents should strive for some common ground and compromise," according to Samalin. They should also be able to count on each other for support in specific instances. Children are quick to spot and take advantage of policy splits. ("Dad said no; let's go ask Mom.") Even if parents do not agree exactly about the handling of every issue, usually it is best not to contradict each other or undermine the absent parent in front of the child. ("Daddy was wrong. He shouldn't have said that to you.") Unless your spouse is abusing the child in some way, according to Samalin, "try to say to yourself, 'He has his system and I have mine,' and walk out—not play the middle man. Wait and talk to him in the bedroom later."

Looking Backward

As discussed in chapter 3, parents will find it helpful to look critically at their own upbringing, to identify which parental policies they would want to repeat with their own children, and which they would not want to replicate. Discussing childhood experiences with each other is one way parents can spot possible conflicts in child-rearing philosophy, even before they have children. Try to remember what the rules were in your family and how they were enforced and also how you felt about them. You may also want to talk about specific issues that sometimes cause conflict in families, such as behavior at mealtimes, bedtime rituals, chores, television, homework, rewards, and punishments.

For some parents, however, such discussions are meaningless in the absence of children. "It's easy to set a firm policy on tantrums over a glass of wine with your husband," one mother says. "It's much harder to carry it out when you're exhausted after a long day and your child is thrashing around on the floor of a crowded toy store."

Traditionally, child-rearing practices—good and bad— were passed on from parent to child. Today's parents are luckier. Books about child-rearing abound and many communities offer parenting courses. There are many more models available and much more open discussion. Whether parents are trying to resolve their differences in advance or working them out gradually as their children grow, these resources often provide invaluable new options.

Problem Solving for Parents

There are several ways for parents to resolve their disagreements about child rearing. The least effective is to announce, in one veiled form or another, ''You are handling this all wrong and making a mess of it. I know all the answers and I'll show you how it should be done.'' ''Graduates'' of parenting courses are especially vulnerable to this mistake, and may unintentionally alienate their spouses with their zeal. People do not change unless they want to change, and the ''know it all'' sort of message from one's mate is unlikely to make a person want to change.

A better way to influence your spouse is to suggest gently and nonjudgmentally (and out of range of the children) an alternative way to handle a particularly thorny situation. ''There's a chapter in this book that helped me handle today's tantrum. Do you want to see it?'' Or ''Maybe we should try not forcing the kids to finish everything on their plates—just let them excuse themselves—and see if they don't eat a reasonable amount. At least we will be able to eat in peace that way.''

Another effective means of persuasion is to model a more desirable behavior. ''I used to demand absolute obedience from my children,'' one mother says. ''I didn't put it in those words, but I would react to their slightest resistance to taking a bath or getting ready for bed with heavy-duty threats. Everything became a battle. Then it dawned on me that this wasn't happening with my husband. He would joke the kids along. Now I try to have a lighter touch, too.''

According to Dr. Thomas Gordon, the psychologist who developed the very successful Parent Effectiveness Training program (P.E.T.), parents often are able to work out their differences successfully with the same problem-solving technique he recommends using with children. Its goal is "mutual agreement," rather than one person winning and the other losing. The six steps of this process, which are elaborated in his book *P.E.T.*, are:

1. Identifying and defining the conflict.
2. Generating possible alternative solutions.
3. Evaluating the alternative solution and eliminating those that are not acceptable to both people.
4. Deciding on the best solution.
5. Working out ways of implementing the solution.
6. Following up to evaluate how it worked.

"For example, some parents disagree about children's allowances. Dad may feel that ten-year-old Megan's allowance should be three dollars per week and should be tied to the completion of certain household chores. But Mom may want to make the point that chores are a child's responsibility as a family member. The allowance, therefore, is separate and should come with no strings attached. They discuss their different beliefs and come up with three possible solutions:. . . ."

1. Megan could receive her $3 free and clear of any conditions.
2. She could receive her $3 only if certain conditions were met.
3. She could receive part of her allowance free and clear and part of it contingent on some set chore.

After some discussion, they decided to raise Megan's allowance to $4—two of which were contingent on her taking out the garbage and walking the dog. After two weeks, they reevaluated the new system and determined that only one change was needed: Instead of walking the dog every afternoon, which turned out to be impractical because it interfered with her after-school activities, Megan opted for one hour's worth of weeding the garden each weekend.

The Myth of the United Front

Dr. Gordon also points out that parents should not expect *always* to be on the same side of every conflict that involves their children. Sometimes they will agree, but at others one parent will be aligned closer to the children than to the other parents. And sometimes all parties may be at odds. Mothers, for instance, generally tend to be more worried about activities that might cause their children physical injury than fathers are. They also generally tend to have higher standards for housekeeping and acceptable dress. Even parents who closely agree about their children's behavior may find that their tolerance is different in certain situations. Both parents who are comfortable about mealtimes at home, for instance, may find that for one parent, formal table manners at a restaurant are much more important.

In problem-solving sessions with their children, each parent should be able to act as a free agent, presenting his or her own needs and feelings. The key to no-lose conflict resolution, according to Dr. Gordon, "is that these differences get worked through until a solution is reached that is acceptable to everyone."

Parents who pretend to accept behaviors merely to keep a united front usually do more harm than good. Children quickly pick up their true feelings through nonverbal cues and feel the disapproval. After all, a child who has lived with his parents for seven years knows exactly how to interpret Mom's raised eyebrow or a twitch of Dad's upper lip. Mixed messages, according to Dr. Gordon, may cause children to distrust their parents. And if these mixed signals are broadcast frequently, children may become anxious and insecure and try to test their parents with their behavior.

Vive la Difference!

Rather than hide their differences, parents can use them to benefit their children and themselves. One mother, for instance, caught herself screaming at her four-year-old daughter every morning before nursery school because she could not tolerate the indecision that went into choosing the right outfit. The solution she found was to have her more relaxed husband take over the job of getting this little girl dressed while Mom made breakfast for everyone. In another family, the father got extremely upset whenever his children started squabbling. His wife was able to say to him, "Look, my sister and I fought all the time and we grew up fine. This isn't really so terrible."

"You can be allies without being carbon copies of each other," Nancy Samalin points out. And ideally, parents' strengths and weaknesses will complement each other; their tolerances and intolerances will balance.

Children also benefit indirectly from their parents' differences, by seeing a wide range of acceptable emotions and points of view. As pediatrician and child development expert Dr. T. Berry Brazelton writes in *Toddlers and Parents*, ''I am sure that a child needs very different treatment from his two parents, although they should, and can, agree fundamentally. With two people for the child to play off, to imitate, and to identify with, the potential for future development is surely enriched.'' By seeing the way you and your spouse react differently to the same situation and, more importantly, how you reach a joint decision, your child will learn and internalize the value of negotiation, compromise, and teamwork.

CHAPTER NINE

•••••

Rules for Siblings

Discipline problems?'' said a father of three. ''We wouldn't have any if we didn't have to keep our children from killing each other.'' He was exaggerating, but not wildly. Researchers in one Canadian study found that 29 percent of the interactions between siblings were hostile.

Sibling relationships, however, involve much more than just fighting, according to Dr. Judy Dunn, a developmental psychologist and author of *Sisters and Brothers*. ''Children act toward their siblings as friends, supporters, comforters, and sympathetic playmates, and not only as bullies and aggressors.'' She also cites a study of a large number of five and six year olds, in which most of the children said they preferred having a sibling to being without one and 73 percent even said they wanted another one.

For better or worse, most children (80 percent in the United States), *do* grow up with siblings. And relationships with siblings are usually the most enduring of their lifetimes, outlasting those with parents and predating those with spouses and children. Some brothers and sisters find comfort and joy in their bond as they grow older. Others continue to fight the battles of childhood. One octogenarian, for instance, still resents his brother for having gotten the favored job in their father's business, though both the business and the father are long since gone.

In the Beginning

Most experts attribute the battles between brothers and sisters to a natural and inevitable competition for the exclusive love of their parents. Chilling accounts of sibling rivalry go back as far as the Bible—to Cain and Abel, Jacob and Esau, Joseph and his brothers—and its intensity is undiminished to the present day. One mother recalled the words of her four year old, a few months after the birth of a sister: "Mommy," she said, "would you be mad at me if I killed Robin?"

Sometimes the make-up of a particular family also contributes to the conflict. Children, though sharing many of the same genes, can still be born with very different temperaments. In school, the quiet, sensitive boy might choose to avoid the loud, rough boy in his class. If they are brothers and are sharing a bedroom, he will not have that choice. Likewise, a very neat child may have to share a room with a slob, who happens to be her sister. The sex of the children may also affect how well they get along. In the early years, according to Dr. Dunn, there is more hostility between siblings of different sexes.

Many experts believe that rivalry is more intense when there is too small a difference in age between siblings. Dr. Burton White, in *The First Three Years of Life*, strongly encourages parents to wait at least three years between children. To very young children, attention equals love, and they are likely to fight—literally—for that attention. After the age of three, however, children have more independence and self-control. They have outside friends and interests that will keep them out of direct competition with a baby.

Parents are also an important factor in sibling rivalry.

They can treat their children and arrange their family lives in ways that foster a minimum of friction and a maximum of affection.

Getting Started on the Right Foot

For firstborn children especially, the birth of a new baby is a very powerful emotional experience. And most firstborns feel ambivalent about the new arrival. On one hand, they are likely to be very curious about the strange new creature in their house. But they are also likely to be upset at the attention it requires and receives. They may act equally ambivalent—by being sweet and friendly to the baby one minute and intentionally upsetting the baby the next. Some children regress to babyish behaviors themselves (wetting their pants, sucking their thumbs, asking for a bottle). Many become tearful and clingy or naughty to gain attention. One mother remembers that every time she sat down to nurse her new baby, "my four-year-old daughter would ask me to do something that takes two hands, like tie her shoe."

How children react to a new baby depends greatly on their individual temperaments. In the "New York Longitudinal Study," which studied children's temperament and which is discussed at length in chapter 2, Drs. Chess and Thomas found that children who are generally positive, mild, and adaptable are less likely to have trouble with any change, including the birth of a sibling, than those who are negative, intense, or slow to adapt to new experiences.

Parents can ease the situation, however, by being especially sensitive to the feelings of the older child. While it is tempting to dote on an adorable new baby, this should not be done at the expense of the first child. (Visitors, too, should be alerted to this.) Parents can be tolerant of babyish behaviors, while emphasizing how exciting it is to be grown up. As the older child works out her feelings, however, parents must protect the baby from being hurt. The best way to do this is not to push the older siblings away but to teach them how to be gentle. Many big brothers and sisters take pride in being able to help feed, bathe, or entertain their babies.

Children as young as two years old are also interested in the feelings of their siblings. By encouraging the older child's empathy for the newcomer, parents can help the older and younger children to develop a caring relationship. They can talk to the older child about what the baby may need or be feeling ("Do you think she's crying because the doorbell scared her?"); they can comment on the baby's interest in the sibling ("She laughs every time you make that funny face!").

Parents can also help by directly acknowledging their children's feelings. In his book *Between Parent and Child* the late Dr. Haim Ginott, a child psychologist and author of many books for parents, gave this example of a mother preparing her daughter for a new baby:

Sometimes he will be fun, but sometimes he will be trouble. Sometimes he will cry and be a nuisance to all of us. He'll wet the crib, make in his diapers, and he will stink. Mother will have to wash him, feed him, and take care of him. You may feel left out. You may feel jealous. You may even say to yourself, "She does not love me anymore—she loves the baby." When you feel that way, *be sure* to come and tell me, and I'll give you extra loving, so you won't have to worry. You'll know that I love you.

Special Treatment

Dr. Ginott also gave parents the key to reducing sibling rivalry: "To each child, let us convey the uniqueness of our relationship, not its fairness and sameness." One way to do this is to set time aside regularly to spend with each child alone. This is obviously more difficult for working parents and for parents of large families. One mother of four manages to follow a special breakfast ritual. One morning a week, she takes each child out for a meal alone with Mom.

Parents who get caught in the trap of trying to treat their children equally soon discover that siblings are never satisfied. Give two sisters identical bracelets, and they will find a flaw to fight over. By treating children as the distinct individuals they are, however, you can sidestep this competition. On one level, this may mean giving one girl a bracelet and the other a baseball bat. On another, it means searching out their special talents and encouraging them, rather than herding the whole family onto the baseball field because that was the choice of the number one child.

Children of different ages also should have different responsibilities and privileges. Older children usually stay up later, get larger allowances, and travel more freely in the neighborhood. Parents can present this to younger children as something to look forward to, rather than as something to resent. They can also remind them of all the exciting advances they have made already.

Respecting children's individuality includes respecting their right to their own possessions and helping them to protect them. If children don't have their own rooms, they can still have separate cabinets or storage shelves. A child with a brother or sister at a particularly destructive age (1½ years, for instance) may even need a lock to protect her possessions.

Parents who cherish their children's differences in these ways will not make the mistake of comparing one to the other and uttering the hateful words some adults still remember: "Why can't you be more like your sister?"

When They Come Out Fighting

There are a number of measures parents can take to contain sibling battles. Most important is setting clear household rules that include forbidding physical and verbal violence. Children should be encouraged instead to express their angry feelings in ways that do not hurt one another—by explaining in words, or by making a No Trespassing sign, for example.

If you can identify the times when your children are most likely to fight, you can separate them in advance. Some children are able to play happily for only an hour. Others get tired and cranky at certain times of the day and will provoke fights or be particularly sensitive then. In general, older children tend to feel most competitive when their younger siblings are the center of attention. Younger children suffer most when their older siblings are advancing and getting new privileges—when they first go to school, for instance.

In their book *Siblings without Rivalry*, Adele Faber and Elaine Mazlish encourage parents to ignore their children's normal bickering and to intervene only when necessary. The most helpful way to intervene, they write, is to

1. Acknowledge the children's anger. ("You two sound really mad at each other!")
2. Reflect each child's point of view. ("So, Sara, you want

to keep holding the puppy. And you, Billy, think you're entitled to a turn, too.'')

3. Describe the problem with respect. (''This is tough. We have two children and only one puppy.'')
4. Express faith in their ability to work it out together. (''I know that you two can find a solution that's fair to each of you and to the puppy.'')
5. Leave.

There are times, however, when parents have to intervene forcefully—when there is verbal or physical abuse, when the problem is disrupting the whole household, or when the same problem keeps recurring. With younger children, the best solution may be a time-out, separating them for several minutes. With older children, the solution may be to call a family meeting to discuss the problem after each has cooled off alone. In any case, according to Faber and Mazlish, ''We intervene, not for the purpose of settling their argument or making a judgment, but to open the blocked channels of communication so that they can go back to dealing with each other.''

In sibling disputes, the best policy is to refuse to take sides. Usually by the time parents arrive it is impossible to assign guilt confidently anyway. Those who do often make the mistake of always blaming the older child. Yet by the age of two, many younger siblings are already skillful at irritating their older sisters and brothers and also at manipulating their parents with tears. One woman claims that her parents ''created sibling rivalry'' between her and her brother, who was 5½ years younger. ''Whenever he destroyed my things, I was supposed to be old enough to understand. If I ever did something to him, I was too old to be acting that way.''

One positive measure you can take to prevent sibling

fights is to praise and encourage generosity and caring between your children whenever it occurs. "That was such a nice thing to do," a mother might say to a girl who helped her little brother write his name on a drawing. "He's really lucky to have a sister like you."

The Silver Lining

Although sibling relationships may be hard on the parents, experts have identified many ways in which they benefit the children. In the safety of their families, children can test a wide range of emotions and behavior without the fear of losing love. They can also develop valuable skills for getting along with other people—how to share, win and lose well, assert themselves, resolve conflicts, love and deal with unloving feelings, and, finally, how to be a friend.

Siblings can also spur a child's intellectual development. When younger children try to imitate their older brothers and sisters, they play in a more mature way than they would on their own. Older siblings may enjoy the role of teacher and gain in self-esteem.

According to Dr. Dunn, the sibling relationship may be an important developmental influence because of its emotional power. "If you compete for parental love with someone," she writes in *Sisters and Brothers*, "it really matters that you should be able to anticipate his or her actions and intentions and to read his or her moods and feelings." Children have displayed powers of understanding in their sibling relationships far beyond those expected for their age. Sometimes they use this understanding to tease their siblings with painful accuracy, but other times they use it to protect and comfort them.

What parents hope for most, perhaps, when they have more than one child is the special bond that can develop between brothers and sisters from their shared family experiences. For parents of squabbling young children, this may seem a distant dream. But based on accounts of adults, the bond usually grows stronger during middle childhood and adolescence.

Help

Although some sibling rivalry is normal and inevitable, it sometimes reaches a pitch that is not. Occasionally the entire relationship between siblings becomes consumed by hatred, jealousy, and intense competition. Fights may be constant and seem never to blow over, so that the children get no pleasure from each other's company. One child may always be abusing the other, physically or verbally.

In these cases, parents may want to seek help from a mental health professional for the child or for the family. Sometimes children express in their fights a stress that the family is experiencing as a whole. Their behavior, for instance, may reflect a long-simmering hostility between their parents.

On the other hand, be careful not to judge your children's behavior too harshly by comparison with that of other children. After all, most sibling battles go on in the privacy of the home. From outside, the family next door will always look more peaceful than your own.

PART III
......
Discipline in Special Situations

"I'm Eddie, one of the demands of single parenthood."

CHAPTER TEN

· · · · · ·

Disciplining the "Difficult" Child

Every parent can spot a "difficult" child. He is firmly planted, screaming, on the nursery-school steps because his mother brought him a chocolate chip cookie instead of an oatmeal one. Or he is flying down the street at top speed in a snowstorm with no overcoat.

As discussed earlier, the pendulum of blame for children's difficult behavior has swung from heredity (bad blood) to environment (including bad parenting, especially bad mothering). Today it seems to have settled in the middle. Most experts believe that parents do not create their child's style of behavior, although they do influence it by their handling.

The "Difficult" Child

Throughout Drs. Chess and Thomas' "New York Longitudinal Study," which is discussed in detail in chapter 2, certain combinations of traits occurred together frequently at each age level, creating three patterns of behavior: the "easy" child, the "slow-to-warm-up" child, and the "difficult" child. Ten percent of the children in their study fell into the difficult pattern. These children had irregular body functions; slow adaptability to change; and intense, often negative, reactions.

In the book *The Difficult Child,* Dr. Stanley Turecki, a child psychiatrist and founder of the Difficult Child Program at Beth Israel Medical Center in New York City, has expanded this definition to include high-activity level, distractibility, and low sensory threshold in the difficult pattern, estimating that he is adding another 5 percent of all children to the difficult group. Among those who need special handling by their parents, he would also include the many more who are basically easy but have some difficult traits.

The Difficult Child stresses that although some of the "normal" child-rearing techniques may not work with these children, the children themselves are all normal. Their parents just need to work harder to understand them and to learn how to manage them.

The Difficulty for Parents

Because of their behavior, difficult children often make their parents feel inadequate, angry, and guilty. One mother who describes her four-year-old daughter as difficult says, "I don't know how we survived the last four years. She didn't sleep through the night until she was three. Then she had tantrums. They weren't worse than other kids, but they were every day and we didn't ever know what would set them off. Recently she was refusing to get dressed for school. I would be yelling and screaming and she would be whining and crying. Now I can really understand child abuse."

Another mother says of her son, whom she describes as a "dervish": "He was frequently a source of embarrassment for me with other children, especially when he fell apart and got aggressive and hit.''

Some parents and children get locked into power struggles. The parent asks the child to do something—to put on his clothes or eat his dinner, for instance—and the child refuses. The parent insists and the child refuses more vehemently. A few more volleys back and forth and a simple request has escalated into a battle royal.

Some parents, fearful or wearied of these contests, give in to their children's demands rather than face their tantrums, thereby creating household tyrants. Other parents, however, worn down by constant misbehavior, are left with a very short fuse. The smallest incident may set them off. "And the more they overreact," writes Dr. Turecki, "the more the child misbehaves. In a sense, the child continues to get even more attention paid to him. Excessive attention, even if it's negative, is such a powerful 'reward' to a child that it actually reinforces the undesirable behavior.''

Difficult children may also cause problems for the family as a whole. Exhausted parents may blame each other for something that is the fault of neither. They may not have enough energy left for their other children, causing anger and jealousy among siblings. Parents of hard-to-handle kids may also not have enough energy for their own needs. Thus weakened, they may be even *less* able to handle their difficult child.

Managing the Difficult Child

"Ineffective discipline," writes Dr. Turecki, "is one of the biggest problems in a family with a difficult child." Often its source is in the blurring of temperamental and nontemperamental behavior and the failure to treat the two types of behavior differently. Some parents punish their child, for example, for behavior that is beyond their child's control and certainly far from any deliberate intention. A very active child who knocks over the tiny glass animals on an end table as he shoots from one end of the room to the other is perhaps no more to blame than the parent who, knowing what this child is like, leaves delicate glassware in his path.

Some parents interpret their children's inability to meet their demands as deliberate defiance. They may, for instance, expect their children to eat meals and go to bed at set times. Children who are irregular by temperament, however, may not be hungry or sleepy at those times. One solution is to separate meal*time* from eating and bed*time* from sleeping. Children may be asked to sit down with the family at dinnertime, but not forced to eat. Instead, a bowl of nutritious snack foods can be set out for later. At bedtime, they may be asked to change into their pajamas and get into bed, but told they can read or play quietly.

Dr. Turecki advises parents to identify the temperamental traits of their children and then to respond differently to behavior that is related to temperament than to behavior that is not. This applies even to outbursts of temper. A child who is having a tantrum because he didn't get seconds on dessert may be trying to manipulate his parents with this behavior. If so, parents can feel confident in being tough—ignoring him, distracting him, or sending him to a time-out. If the tantrum is caused by a temperamental issue (if the child with low adaptability finished his dessert and expected a second helping, for instance), he may be totally out of control. This child should be treated more sympathetically and held until he calms down.

Once parents understand their children's temperaments, they can try to prevent or manage problems. One father says, for example, "We're the kind of household that, by nature, does not have a huge number of rules and regulations, and we didn't learn the necessity for them with our older daughter. But with our son, who always needs to be prepared for what to expect, we've found that setting some things down makes him more comfortable."

For a child with low adaptability, transitions may cause a problem. One mother found that her daughter got very upset whenever she picked her up from playing at a friend's. Now, instead, she calls in advance and asks the friend's parent to bring the child to the car. (Difficult children, like most other children, usually behave better with adults other than their parents.)

With children 2½ years and older, Dr. Turecki also recommends using what he calls a "changing clock." Show the child the time on a digital clock and tell him that when the number on the right becomes a five (or whatever is appropriate) it will be time to change to the next activity.

Parents with children who initially withdraw from anything new should always prepare them for a change in routine. If they are going somewhere unfamiliar, it may help to take along a familiar toy. Although some children may require a long period of slow exposure, parents should not give up. Otherwise, they may deprive the child of important experiences, and the child may not feel the satisfaction of mastering something new.

Very active or intense children may act wild when they get overexcited, behavior that can easily escalate. Vigilant parents can learn to recognize the point when their child's behavior is about to change, and then intervene. One mother, who had always forbade her older son any television during the week, has found that watching television relaxes his more difficult younger brother. In the late afternoons, when he has a friend over and is likely to be wound up, she often brings them a snack and suggests a television show.

Dr. Turecki recommends that with distractible children it is often helpful to make eye contact to get their attention. In fact, this is a standard technique of classroom management. "If we're sitting in a group," one veteran nursery-school teacher says, "and the children seem to be getting too wild, I'll say, 'I want to see all of your eyes,' and I'll look from one to another. And then I'll say their names." Parents can help an older child deal with his own distractibility by offering practical suggestions, such as keeping a list of each day's responsibilities and referring to it regularly.

Some aspects of temperament, however, can only be recognized and accepted. When your child insists that his socks tickle or the grape jam tastes "funny," it may just be that he has sensitive skin or a sensitive palate. Giving him a choice of several kinds of socks or jam may help, and may also serve as a guide to your future choices.

Furthermore, "slow-to-warm-up" children may never satisfy you with suitably enthusiastic responses. One mother says of her daughter, "When she first meets people, she doesn't smile and say 'Hi!' like other kids. She's kind of glum." With this type of child, as with others, what Dr. Turecki calls "labeling" may be helpful. You might say *to yourself*, "This is the way he is; he can't help it." Dr. Turecki also recommends helping children over three years old to label their own traits and thus gain some control over their behavior. "Please don't leave me yet," a child might learn to say to his father at the entrance to a birthday party. "I need a little more time to get used to it here."

Less Discipline, Not More

A family with a difficult child may have a history of failed discipline. The natural response to this failure may be to make more rules and make them tougher. The right response for a difficult child, however, is fewer rules. Such a family may also have tried a number of different approaches and given them up because they were not effective as quickly as they expected them to be. Yet consistency is vitally important with a difficult child.

In starting fresh, you should be certain first that any demands you make on our children are within their ability, considering their temperaments. Then you should decide whether the demands are worth making. Ask yourself, "Is it really important that my child put his napkin on his lap?" "Does it matter if he sleeps in his T-shirt instead of his pajamas?" Make your basic rules of behavior clear and simple and make the punishments clear as well. When you are working to change behavior, work on one issue at a time. Once that is resolved, you can turn to the others.

Difficult children tend to respond better to rewards for good behavior than to punishments for bad behavior. Dr. Turecki sometimes recommends a system of planned rewards. One mother used this technique to stop her son from using unacceptable language: Every day he went without using it, he got a gold star. After 10 gold stars, he could pick out a toy at the dime store. This worked so well, she says, "he even reported when he said a bad word at school."

Finally, in carrying out effective discipline with difficult children, try to resist acting in the heat of the moment. Instead, give yourself time to respond with thought instead of emotion.

Help

Some parents worry that their temperamentally high-activity children have a pathological condition often called hyperactivity. A teacher or another parent may even have suggested this to them. Since the coining of the term, there has been disagreement about where to draw the line between what is normal and what is abnormal. Most experts do agree, however, that hyperactivity involves additional symptoms of an attention disorder. "In this condition," according to Drs. Chess and Thomas, "the very movements are impulsive and accompanied by very short attention span and excessive distractibility. Such a child finds it very hard to sustain his attention in any one direction."

In any case, diagnosing hyperactivity requires experience and training, and should be left to professionals. Once the diagnosis is made, the hyperactive children may need special help. However, many of the same techniques for understanding and handling other difficult children may still be helpful.

But children need not be hyperactive for their parents to seek help. If behavior problems continue after children are five years or so or if problems develop for other members of the family, Dr. Turecki recommends that parents talk with a mental health professional. For preschool children, treatment should focus on helping the parents handle the troublesome behaviors. Elementary-age children may need therapy themselves, which may be fairly brief. The most common problem for these older difficult children is a poor self-image. ("I'm no good"; "I can't do anything right.")

In *Your Child Is a Person,* Drs. Chess and Thomas along with Dr. Herbert Birch offer parents this guideline for when to seek professional help: "Whenever parent-child relations are such that tension is the dominant theme and relaxed enjoyment of the child is increasingly infrequent."

CHAPTER ELEVEN

••••••

Disciplining in Single-Parent Families

Parenthood is a stressful job, even when divided by two," writes Dr. Raymond Guarendi, a clinical psychologist and author of *You're a Better Parent Than You Think!* "But if you're taking on the job alone, you can total all the stresses . . . and multiply them by two for each child you have." The number of parents bearing these stresses has soared in the last 25 years. In 1960, according to the Census Bureau, only 1 child in 10 lived in a single-parent household. By 1986, the figure was 1 in 4. And now the bureau estimates that as many as 6 children in 10 will spend at least some time living with a single parent before they are 18 years old.

Most single parents are separated (24 percent), divorced (42 percent), or widowed (7 percent). And most of them (89 percent) are women. Twenty-seven percent never married. Of those, a few are single mothers by choice, but many are adolescent girls, totally unprepared to be parents and breadwinners.

Even in the best circumstances, however, it is difficult to raise children alone. "It's hard being the only decision maker," says the divorced mother of an 11 year old, "because you're never sure you're right. It must be really nice to be able to say to your husband, 'What do you think we should do about this?' " Furthermore, supplies of time, energy, and money are usually stretched thin for single parents. And those who are newly divorced or widowed may have to try to sustain their parenting role while floundering in a sea of intense emotions, both their own and their children's.

Although single parents can apply effectively the same philosophy of child rearing as married parents do, some areas of discipline may be more difficult for them. In fact, many of the single parents who seek professional help complain of problems with disciplining their children.

The Newly Single Parent

Experts recommend that as much as possible newly single parents maintain the rules of behavior they set in the past for their children as well as the familiar routines for mealtimes, bedtimes, and chores. This household structure gives children a sense of security in their radically changed and usually frightening new world.

Unfortunately, right after a separation or death is just when providing structure is hardest to do. Both parents and children are likely to be shaken by feelings of sorrow, fear, and anger. One mother describes herself when she was first separated as "totally overwhelmed. I felt alone, inadequate, frustrated, and panicky. I had nightmares about every decision I made. I felt I just couldn't do it all, and my child was running me in circles."

Children, for their part, may respond to the crisis with a variety of symptoms, ranging from depression and withdrawal to regression and extreme misbehavior. The newly single parent may be too preoccupied to handle these symptoms appropriately. She may allow a child to abuse her verbally or physically, for instance, when she should be encouraging the child to talk about her anger instead. The parent may say yes just because she doesn't have the energy to say no firmly enough. She may be so grateful to a child who is suddenly unnaturally well behaved that she misses the child's message ("I'd better be good or she'll send me away, too") and, therefore, puts a frightened child in an even more frightening position. A newly single father who had always kept his children at a distance may need time to develop a nurturing style.

In *Surviving the Breakup*, their study of how children and parents cope with divorce, Drs. Judith Wallerstein and Joan Kelly emphasize how important it is for the custodial parent to rebound from her distress. "The central hazard which divorce poses to the psychological health and development of children and adolescents," they write, "is in the diminished or disrupted parenting which so often follows in the wake of the rupture and which can become consolidated within the postdivorce family."

Avoiding the Pitfalls

Dr. Guarendi calls guilt "possibly the most corrosive destroyer of parental authority in one-parent households." Newly single parents, who often have low self-esteem, can find many reasons to feel guilty: They feel that they failed at their marriage; they may have let their children see or overhear vicious arguments before or during the separation; they believe they have deprived their children of a parent; they have to work long hours and see too little of their children; and they can no longer afford to buy their children whatever they want. To make up to their children for this suffering, some single parents tend to be overindulgent. As one divorced mother says, ''I kept getting this panicked feeling that I was going to ruin the rest of my daughter's life if I said no to anything.''

People who feel they have just lost the love of their spouse also may worry about losing the love of their children if they demand too much of them. Ideally, the ex-spouse would support the custodial parent's household rules. But some, instead, encourage an unhealthy competition, either because of anger left over from the divorce or because of their own feelings of guilt toward the children. Both parents may then vie to win their children's love with favors.

Children are quick to take advantage of these situations. ''At Daddy's house, we get to stay up till midnight.'' Or ''It wouldn't be so bad when you're at work if we could at least watch television.'' In reality, the child may be yearning for someone to set some limits in a world turned topsy-turvy.

The emotional, physical, and financial burdens of single parenthood—the ''always ongoing weariness,'' as one divorced mother describes it—also can take their toll on discipline. ''I am sometimes so overstressed with demands,'' one single mother says, ''that it is easier to say yes than no. Other times I am overly harsh because I don't have the patience. I want instant obedience because I can't take any more problems.''

Parents do their children no favor by easing up on rules or by being inconsistent. Children who are given no limits tend to lose control of themselves, and their misbehavior can be seen as a plea for discipline.

To avoid these pitfalls, single parents need first to recognize them, then to build their strength as parents by taking care of *themselves* as people. One conclusion of a recent forum on the single-parent family in the journal *Family Relations* was that "the well-being of the single parent after the divorce is a major factor in stabilization and the subsequent adjustment of the children." As their custodial parent begins to make a new life for herself, children get the message that now everything is going to be all right.

Single parents should try to reserve time for just themselves, even if it is time they would otherwise be spending with their children. They need to pursue interests and relationships. For those single parents for whom a job is not a financial necessity it still may be a psychological one; work may provide a source of self-esteem, a social life, and an escape from the withering demands of child care. Finally, single parents may have to learn to be satisfied with a house that is not spotless and with meals that are less than gourmet.

Shared Responsibility

Some of the problems of working single custodial parents are simply the result of understaffing. There is just as much to be done as before, but less time and less help to do it. Even fathers who did little housework usually contributed at least baby-sitting time to the upkeep of the household.

Fortunately, children can be recruited to help fill the gap to the benefit of the whole family. "All children should have chores," according to Dr. William Koch, a child development specialist and director of the "Skhool" for Parents in New York City. "That's part of living in the house and part of learning how to take care of yourself. Children actually like responsibility. They may grumble about it, but they will feel good about being part of the family and accomplishing things.'' One six-year-old girl who takes out the garbage, sets and clears the table, and is learning how to make her bed refused her little brother's offer to help. ''That's my job,'' she insisted.

Children usually take pride in having an important role in the running of the house and in being able to do something meaningful for their parents. Children also take pride in learning some of the practical skills of housekeeping and money management. And families that work together at solving these problems often develop a special closeness and sensitivity to each other's needs.

In families where children have not been asked to participate at home before, it may be best to introduce the idea at a family meeting. The single parent can explain her need for help and express her gratitude for her children's cooperation.

Parents with experience sharing chores offer three tips:

1. Give precise instructions. Rather than saying ''Clean up your room,'' ask the child to make the bed, empty the hamper, and pick up the books and toys.
2. Children who choose what they want to do are more likely to do it well.
3. Switch jobs frequently (once a week with young children) to prevent boredom.

Although children as young as three can share in housework, responsibilities should be appropriate to the child's age and not so burdensome that they interfere with play or schoolwork. Three year olds can be asked to keep their toys in order and dress themselves, for instance. Four and five year olds can learn how to make their beds, and a five year old could help with the dishes. An eight year old is old enough to vacuum or clean the kitchen and some 10 year olds are ready to help prepare meals. Some children enjoy being able to take care of younger siblings. Parents need to be certain, however that their children's pleasure is in nurturing, not just in bossing their siblings around.

Parents should also be particularly careful not to deprive their children of their childhoods by treating them as little adults. ''Using the child as a confidant or saying to a little boy, 'You're going to be the man of the house now' is frightening,'' Dr. Koch points out. ''Children need to know that they are going to be protected and taken care of, that it is not their responsibility to suddenly start taking care of mommy's needs.''

Shared Decision Making

For single-parent families, many experts recommend a democratic style of management, a style of shared decision making. It seems natural that children who share the household responsibilities will also want to at least take part in making household decisions and setting rules. And because a single parent is dependent on her children's cooperation, she will want the rules to be ones they understand and accept. A preteen, for example, is more likely to respect a curfew she has had a voice in setting than one that is imposed on her without discussion.

At family meetings, parents and children may talk about any family issue—the content and timing of meals, planning a vacation at the beach, complaints about siblings, homework problems, and television rules, as well as the assignment of chores. Children should be encouraged to help set the agenda.

Single parents who try to share decisions probably accommodate more to their children's wishes than they might if a second parent were present. They probably also are asking more of their children than they would in a two-parent household. Shared decision making, however, need not be pure democracy. A parent can guarantee her children that she will consider their opinions on every issue, while also warning them that some decisions will be hers alone to make.

Like taking responsibility for doing chores, participating in decision making is a growth experience for children and one that draws a family together. Often children in single-parent families seem more self-reliant and mature than other children their age and feel a strong sense of common cause with the other members of their family.

Seeking Help When You Need It

For their own and their children's sake, single parents should not neglect their own emotional well-being. Many people draw strength from support groups for single parents run by community organizations and also nationally by Parents without Partners. These groups may fulfill a range of needs: providing speakers on topics of child development, forums for sharing experiences, or social opportunities to meet other single parents and children.

Some parents may need individual help from a mental health professional for themselves or their children. One divorced mother who is seeing a therapist with her daughter says, "I kept catching myself screaming at her and I could see that she was afraid. I was worried that I was ruining my wonderful child.''

The kind of help working single parents probably need most, however, is social support, in the form of improved and readily available child care.

CHAPTER TWELVE

......

Disciplining in Stepfamilies

Not long ago, the topic of how to discipline a stepchild would have appeared in a book on child care only as a footnote. Most readers would have spared it a brief glance and a ho hum. But now, since the rise in the number of divorces beginning in the late 1960s, what was once a fine point of parenting is a critical concern for many men and women. National statistics from 1985 show that 18.8 percent of married couples with children include at least one stepchild, meaning that there are more than 4.5 million custodial stepparents and an uncounted number of noncustodial stepparents.

New Roles, New Rules

Today's stepparents who come from intact families are unprepared for many of the situations they will encounter. Their primary role models for how to raise children (their own parents) are often not appropriate. One stepmother describes how even now that she is 36 years old, her own mother often surprises her with special little gifts. Yet when she bought handsome polo shirts for her new visiting stepsons, they tossed them in a closet and never looked at them again. "What we have in no way resembles the family I grew up in," she says.

Unlike intact families, remarried families are composed of people with very uneven relationships. The parent has a natural bond with the children enriched by years of nurturing; the parent and new spouse have a love so deep they chose to marry; the stepparent, however, often has only an acquaintance with the children; and the children often have suspicions and fears of the new family member.

Remarried families are also complicated by the sheer number of interested parties—"Us, the Ex, the Ex's Mate, the New Mate's Ex, and the Kids," as Delia Ephron describes them in the subtitle of her book *Funny Sauce.* What this may feel like to children is a lot more grown-ups bossing them around.

For remarried families where one or both spouses were widowed, a whole other set of issues come into play: The stepparent may feel the obligation to compete with the memory of the deceased parent to gain acceptance from the child. And in addition to all the usual rigors of parenting, the newly merged family has to find a way to come to terms with the complexities of death.

But whether remarriage is preceeded by death or divorce, normal child-rearing issues, especially in the early years of a remarriage, can become very highly charged. While most of the discord in first marriages has been found to revolve around money and sex, in stepfamilies the key source of stress is the children. And this stress takes a toll. A recent study reported that 17 percent of remarriages with stepchildren on both sides ended in divorce within three years. The figure for divorces without stepchildren was 10 percent.

The issue of discipline, which is one of the toughest issues for intact families, is intensified in remarriages. But it is not insoluble. In fact, stepparents can use successfully the same approaches to discipline described earlier in this book. At first there may be differences in who should apply the discipline, how, and when. But once family relationships are stable, the goal in most custodial families is for both parents to be equal partners in making rules and enforcing them.

The Virtue of Patience

Experts almost universally counsel stepparents to wait. Stepfamilies are "instant" families only in the sense that they are created legally at the instant of remarriage. In fact, becoming a family that thinks of itself as "we" and that accepts the stepparent as an equal partner is a long-term process. Although some families blend faster or more slowly than others, it usually takes at least 18 months to two years.

This adjustment period is a time for the stepparent to get to know the children and to develop a relationship of respect and trust. After all, biological parents spend almost two years nurturing their children before discipline becomes an issue. In stepfamilies, it is usually best, at first, for the biological parent to continue handling discipline, especially the enforcing of rules. The stepparent can then focus on nurturing. This is particularly helpful to noncustodial stepparents, who usually spend very little time with the child.

In the hothouse of stepfamily relations, there are many potential sources of conflict. Arguments over whether the spaghetti should have meat sauce or meatballs have turned into holy wars. Sometimes these arguments stem from the natural human preference for keeping things the way they have always been. But they may also reflect deeper issues for the child, and require sensitive handling.

One seven year old informed his stepmother, who liked to set a formal table for dinner, that in his mother's house, where he lived, he ate on paper plates—and that was the better way. Realizing that this little boy was feeling disloyal to his mother for having what he called a "fancy" dinner with her, the stepmother offered to compromise. "Okay," she said, "one week we'll use the china, one week we'll use the paper plates."

While stepparents should be flexible, they don't have to be doormats. They have a right to protect their own interests and preferences. One stepmother describes the pattern her husband originally set up for the weekends when his daughter visited, "I would cook and clean and he would take her to the movies. I was also supposed to leave so that they could spend private time together. Finally it just got too cold to sit and read in the park." Another stepmother described a camping trip she took with her husband and stepchildren. "We got out of the car and everyone ran off to do what they wanted—fish, swim, whatever. I was left to get the food ready. I got really angry. 'I'm on this trip to have fun, too,' I said, 'and that's just not fair.'"

What is most important is that new stepparents not move in and immediately try to whip everyone into shape, or give the impression that that is what they have in mind. Those who do often find themselves slipping into the stereotypes of the "wicked stepmother" or the "cruel stepfather."

They may also find that they have incurred the resentment not only of their stepchildren but of their spouses as well. Like mother bears, biological parents have a natural instinct to run to the defense of their children when they are being attacked. Although they may have encouraged the new spouse to share parenting responsibilities, they may not be ready for any faultfinding at first. One stepfather describes how he learned to discipline his stepson indirectly. "It isn't such a good idea for Josh to drink soda for breakfast, is it?" he might say to his wife. With his own son, he would just have taken away the can of soda.

Criticism at the beginning, if given at all, should be delivered with velvet gloves. Rather than demanding, "Clean up your room right now!" the stepparent could say, "I see it has gotten pretty messy in here. If you like, I could give you a hand putting your things away."

In a stepfamily, as in a biological family, discipline does not work if it is based solely on a fear of punishment. The child who perceives his stepfather or stepmother as a friendly, caring adult in his life will be much more willing to cooperate with family rules. Generally a stepchild will respond best to discipline measures if there is an existing foundation of a positive relationship with the stepparent.

To make friends with a stepchild, it is not necessary to bring home a new doll or video game every night. Children appreciate the value of time spent together. Play a game of checkers or throw a ball in the backyard. If you take your stepchildren along on an errand, surprise them with ice cream cones. Build a history for your new family of shared trips and special celebrations. One stepmother remembers winning over her stepdaughter when she supported her negotiations for a higher allowance. A stepfather was able to connect with his stepson through their mutual interest in football, an interest the boy's natural father didn't share.

There is another side of the relationship equation that is often overlooked and that is that real, caring relationships take time to develop. "When I make my own son straighten up his room," one stepmother explains, "I'm not doing it just so the room will be clean. I want to teach him responsibility. With my stepson, at first, I didn't have that kind of investment.''

Who Makes the Rules?

Even before the marriage, partners in a new stepfamily, can take steps to avoid conflicts over discipline. Elizabeth Einstein, author of *The Stepfamily*, recommends that each parent identify his own style of discipline and where there are differences, work out a compromise. Biological parents do this naturally, over time, as their children grow and as discipline issues come up. But stepparents do not have that luxury. Issues will come up immediately and they will have to act.

For stepfamilies, Einstein recommends a democratic style of discipline, in which the children take part in setting the rules and the consequences. ''The outcome of the democratic style,'' she writes, ''is that it promotes communication and respect within the family and raises the children's level of self-esteem. And this approach to parenting fosters self-discipline within the children and creates a relaxed, comfortable atmosphere in which the new stepfamily can flourish.''

Some stepfamilies hold regular family meetings to discuss plans, rules, and grievances. These work especially well for teenagers and in blended families, with two sets of children. In some families, no action is taken unless there is a consensus. In others, while everyone has a voice, some decisions are reserved for the adults.

Parents whose children are too young for family meetings (usually under five) or who prefer a more authoritarian style can still benefit from discussing their differences and compromising on rules that both agree are fair. By setting rules in advance about eating habits, hygiene, living space, and household chores (all common sources of conflict in stepfamilies), they can avoid many problems. And the fewer rules and more choices children in a stepfamily have, the easier discipline will be.

After the general rules are set, the natural parent can present them to the children as gently as possible. A father might say, for instance, "Now that there are more of us, we're going to have to make certain rules more clear in the family so that everybody can understand what kind of things are expected of them."

Ideally, expectations for children in the homes where they live and the ones that they visit would be similar or at least not contradictory. On the other hand, neither parent should be bound by the rules of the other just for the sake of consistency. After all, children are used to adjusting to different standards of behavior—at school, at Grandma's, and at home.

After a divorce, it is important not to undermine the rules of the other home. There is nothing more painful to children with divorced parents than listening to one criticize the other. ("That's just like your father to let you watch the football game all night when he knew you had an exam. He never did care about your education!")

After a parent's death, particularly if it was recent, children may idealize the past and claim that there didn't *used* to be friction or discipline issues. ("My real father would have never yelled at me like you did. My father never got angry at me.") Bear in mind that this kind of exaggeration is a method of preserving positive memories, and of remaining "loyal" to the deceased parent, and should not be interpretted as a personal affront to the stepparent.

What's Normal?

One handicap stepparents have is a serious information gap. Because they weren't part of their stepchildren's past, they can't recognize, at first, patterns of behavior and deviations. What looks like misbehavior to the stepparent may have been perfectly acceptable behavior in the nuclear family.

Also, like all parents, stepparents need to be able to see their children's behavior in the perspective of normal child development. A two year old who throws a tantrum when his stepmother tries to button his snow jacket before he goes out in the freezing cold may be acting like a two year old, not like a stepson. A preteen who communicates in rude grunts may be acting like a twelve year old, not a stepdaughter. One stepmother of grunting teenage boys made this discovery by comparing notes with a neighbor. She describes her relief, "At first I was convinced these kids were just trying to make me crazy."

For this reason, stepparents who helped bring up their own younger siblings, have children of their own, or have worked with children often have an advantage. One stepmother who inherited children 10, 12, and 15 years old relied on skills she learned as a junior-high-school remedial-reading teacher. "Within the context of work," she said, "I focused on personal self-concept development as a way to help them learn. I had this in my general bag of tricks and knew how to deal with discipline-problem kids and kids in general." Nevertheless, before she got married she decided to take a parenting course.

Children's age also affects how well they are apt to accept a stepparent. Experts agree that generally the younger the child is, the easier the adjustment will be. Elementary-age children are more flexible and they also need more help from adults. They can see the benefit of having a more settled household and an additional parent figure.

Adolescents, however, are hard on their parents and even harder on new stepparents. In a sense, the two have opposing interests. The stepparent wants to pull the family closer and to establish a role of authority. Yet adolescents, in order to establish their own identity, tend to challenge authority and break away from their families.

Like first-time parents, stepparents should try to learn as much as they can about normal child development, either from reading books or attending parenting groups. Many experts also recommend getting advice and preparation from a mental health professional who specializes in stepfamilies.

Understanding Death and Divorce

Another handicap for many stepparents is the emotional state of the members of their new family, some of whom may not yet have recovered completely from the death or divorce. Because of unresolved feelings, the children may be unwilling to accept the stepparent, and the natural parent may have created a confusing discipline situation.

In *Surviving the Breakup*, Drs. Wallerstein and Kelly identify some emotions children experience when their parents get divorced. First, they state, children are frightened and feel more vulnerable in a world that now seems much less reliable to them. They worry about their parents, who are upset, and they worry about their own future. Because their parents tend to be preoccupied with their own feelings, children may feel rejected and lonely. Children also feel anger, an emotion that may later be projected on a new stepparent.

Most children of divorce feel torn between their two parents. Their conflict of loyalty may be intensified by a stepparent who makes the mistake of trying to take over the parent's role, or by an absent parent who feels threatened. "I've always thought Tim's father had a lot at stake in our not getting along," one stepfather says.

Because of their terrible sense of loss, many children of divorced parents cling to the fantasy that their parents will reunite. Stepparents are obviously an unwelcome obstacle. One child did away with her stepmother and stepsister in a dream she told her father about: Their house burned down and everyone was killed except the two of them.

Children's reactions to the stepparent are also affected by the relationship they have with their custodial parent, usually the mother. After a divorce, some children become especially close to their mothers and may fear that they are being replaced in her affections. Some, who have had to take on new responsibilities, may not want to give up their grown-up roles to a stepparent, seen as an interloper.

Some parents let standards of discipline slip during the divorce period because they are afraid of losing their children's love to the other parent, or they may feel guilty for what their children have suffered, or they just may not have the emotional energy. Noncustodial parents may become "sugar daddies," full of guilt at leaving their children and unwilling to spoil their brief time together with discipline.

What the stepparent may inherit from the divorce, then, are fears, resentments, and potential power struggles.

Growing into the Stepparent Role

Being a stepparent, especially at the beginning, is often hard, thankless labor. You may feel that you have all the everyday responsibilities of a biological parent but none of the rewards. Biological parents do not expect to be thanked for making beds or paying bills. Their rewards are in watching the children they love thrive and grow. Stepparents *do* need to be thanked, if not by the children, then by their spouses.

Many new stepparents, however, are not only unappreciated but abused by their stepchildren. "It was as if I was invisible," says one stepmother. "If the sugar was in front of me and Tom was way across at the other end of the table, Molly would turn to him and say, 'Daddy, please get me the sugar,' " Another stepmother was terribly hurt by her stepdaughter's hostile assertion that "things were better before you came." But she "kept right on doing all the parenting things. I made her nice meals, I took her to school, I picked her up. I fulfilled my role and responsibility. It's hard to stay angry at someone who's doing things for your benefit."

During the early period when only the biological parent may be enforcing rules, there will still be times when the stepparent has to assert authority. If a child is in danger of hurting himself—by running into the street or bouncing around in the back of the car, for instance—the stepparent has to act immediately. When the biological parent is away, the stepparent may have to discipline the child. Before leaving, however, the biological father or mother should explain to the child directly that the stepparent now has his or her authority to enforce the rules.

If the child misbehaves and then says to the stepparent

(as many children do), "You're not my mommy. I don't have to do what you say," an appropriate response might be, "You're right. I'm not your mommy. But I'm the grown-up in charge now, and I'm reminding you of the rules."

Sometimes stepparents, especially noncustodial stepparents, are left alone with the children before they feel ready to be the actual enforcers of the rules. If so, they could say to a child who has misbehaved, "I'm very unhappy about what just happened. We'll need to talk with Dad about it when he comes back."

In order to discipline, when the time comes, the stepparent needs to have the parent's unconditional support. Even in an intact family, if children suspect there is disagreement between their parents, they will play one off the other. This is more true in a stepfamily, where the children may feel they have something to gain by weakening the stepparent's authority.

Usually stepparents move gradually from being mere advisers to the biological parent about the child and taking no direct role in discipline to being able to make discipline decisions spontaneously. However long this takes, it represents a great achievement: the development of a bond of trust and mutual respect between stepparent and child.

The Myth of Instant Love

Some stepparents want more than mutual respect from their stepchildren. They want to love and be loved—an unrealistic expectation that plagues many stepfamilies. Even in the ideal situation, stepparents cannot help feeling differently about their natural children and their stepchildren. And children cannot help feeling differently about their biological parents. As many children have said themselves, "I don't need three parents."

In combined families, the goal is not equal feelings but equal treatment. "I try to make it so that there's no difference," says a stepfather who also has a child from his previous marriage. "Sometimes this comes naturally. Sometimes it takes a concerted effort to make sure." Stepparents can be frank about this with their stepchildren. "I don't know you as well as my own kids," a stepparent might say. "There may be times that I hurt your feelings or do something you don't like without realizing it. I want you to let me know when that happens."

Yet the relationship between stepparent and stepchild may become one of love, and even if not, it can be rewarding, as Cherie Burns writes in *Stepmotherhood*, "It's not a mother-daughter relationship, and we're not sisters either. But we meet on common ground. We've shared troubles, good times, even loved ones. That means a lot. When you do get a sign of affection from a stepchild, it's just great because you know they didn't have to do it."

Stepparents also play an important part, along with the natural parents, in shaping children's psychological, social, and moral development. Even noncustodial stepparents serve as role models for their stepchildren through their behavior.

Help!

Now that their numbers have grown, stepfamilies no longer have to struggle alone. Some parents and stepparents benefit from support groups, such as those conducted nationwide by the Stepfamily Association of America (602 E. Joppa

Rd., Baltimore, MD 21204). Many stepparents are relieved to discover that their experiences and feelings are normal. "I got the courage to tell my husband how I felt," says one participant, "after I heard other people saying the same things."

With a perspective of normal stepfamily life, it is also possible to spot signs of deeper trouble. Any child who suddenly becomes a behavior problem may be calling out for professional help. Young children may also become withdrawn or hostile or develop persistent illnesses. Older children may get into trouble at school, drink, or take drugs.

Many counselors who work with stepfamilies recommend that the partners come in even before their marriage to learn about some of the common problems and ways to handle them. Karen Savage, director of the Stepfamily Resource Center in Briarcliff Manor, New York, and author of *The Good Stepmother*, thinks of herself as the "family doctor" for some stepfamilies. They come back to her over time, individually or together, when they need help. "A stepfamily is a complicated, difficult, and unusual kind of family," she says, "and to consult a family therapist about how to make it best work for your family under your particular circumstances is normal. You don't have to wait until things are at a crisis state."

CHAPTER THIRTEEN

· · · · · ·

Discipline by Other Care Givers

In many families, discipline is an issue not only for the parents. For a few hours or many hours a day, someone else is caring for the children. In the United States, the number of working mothers of young children has soared over the last decade. In 1976, the Census Bureau reported that 21 percent of new mothers stayed in the work force. By 1987, that figure had risen to 50.8 percent. Most experts project that 75 percent of the children born today will have mothers who work full-time for some period during their first four years.

Many factors affect what kind of child care a family chooses—whether in-home care giver or day care; whether part-time, full-time, or occasional. But in every case, a close fit between care giver and parents is the best choice for the child. Dr. Bryna Siegel-Gorelick, a psychologist and author to *The Working Parents' Guide to Child Care*, stresses that ''follow-through on parents' child-rearing philosophy is as necessary an ingredient for a good day-care arrangement as love for the child and eagerness and willingness to do well.''

Choosing the Right Care Giver

"When a family decides to have someone else take care of the children, this is a major decision and major energy has to go into it," according to Peggy Kociubes, child-care coordinator for University Hospital in Boston, Massachusetts. Ideally, parents will first interview several candidates on the phone or visit several child-care centers or family child-care providers. They will then arrange a personal interview and check references.

The main goal of the interviews is to find out whether the care giver shares your ideas about children. On the telephone, you can explore the practical matters of availability and pay, but also be alert to how intelligent people sound and how well they listen to you. You will not want a care giver who says yes to everything you say and then proceeds with her own agenda. You will also need someone you can trust to make most decisions on her own.

In preparation for personal interviews, first decide what your priorities are. Then set up questions around them. The best questions are neutral and open-ended, ones that will not reveal your bias before the care giver reveals hers and ones that demand more than a yes or no answer. Rather than asking, "How do you discipline?" or "How do you handle a child who does something wrong?" Ms. Kociubes recommends, "Can you tell me how a day would go from 8 o'clock to 5 o'clock?" "What kinds of things do you do?" "What kinds of conflicts come up?" "How do you handle them?" Be careful not to rush in with a second question before the first is fully answered. "It is in that uncomfortable pause period that you get the real meat of it," she says. "That is when revealing things are said." Then ask the care giver for her reaction to some hypothetical situations.

Dr. Sirgay Sanger, author of *You and Your Baby's First Year*, believes that questions of right and wrong are out of place in the first year and thus warns against care givers who describe their former charges as "too demanding" or "spoiled." Ms. Kociubes says, "Whenever I hear from a child-care provider that so-and-so was 'bad,' it concerns me. It means that she sees thing in black and white."

Parents looking for in-home care givers often have to choose between someone who is very young and unformed, willing to accept their ideas but in need of help, and someone older and more experienced, but more set in her ways.

A way to help a younger care giver is to introduce her to someone who can be a role model. "One important lesson a mentor can teach your novice," Dr. Sanger writes in *The Woman Who Works, the Woman Who Cares*, "is how to deal with disciplinary infractions in ways that bring them to an end but still leave your child's dignity intact."

Calling references is usually the last step. Again, use neutral, open-ended questions such as "Can you tell me about your experience with Virginia?" "How did a day go?" "How did she deal with fighting?"

Some parents hire a care giver for a trial period, during which they will be present at least some of the time. You can be sure then that what the care giver said in the interview is what she does. And she can model herself on your style and become familiar with the children. This should ease the adjustment for everyone, and perhaps prevent some discipline problems from occurring. Once the job starts permanently, you should still allow time each day to discuss any problems.

Parents looking for home day care or day-care centers should also make appointments to observe for at least an hour. Dr. Siegel-Gorelick recommends two techniques for effective observation. Either focus on one person at a time (a child or a teacher) for at least five minutes, or "sample events," watching how fights over toys, aggressiveness, or crying are handled.

Your children will probably let you know if you make the wrong choice of care giver. When children are confused by conflicting styles of discipline, they often show it in their behavior. According to Dr. Sanger, "Reappearance of previously overcome misbehavior is the most common indication." On a Saturday, for example, a child might throw sand in the sandbox to see whether her mother responds as she always did or as the care giver does. This problem is more likely to occur in day care because care givers cannot adopt every parent's style. Once it is pointed out, however, they can adjust their responses to soften the difference.

Grandparents as Care Givers

In some families, grandparents, usually grandmothers, help to raise the children. Dr. Benjamin Spock describes some of the advantages in *Raising Children in a Difficult Time*. Admitting his prejudice as a grandparent himself, he writes that most grandparents "feel close enough by blood to their grandchildren to take pride in their accomplishments and delight in their charms, but . . . manage to escape that anxious sense of responsibility they themselves had as parents." Because grandparents are usually less concerned with teaching than parents are and are also less pressed for time, they may offer children a different kind of play, which is both valuable and pleasurable. Their activities together may be more open-ended and less directed.

Some parents fear that the grandparents will "spoil" their children with gifts and indulgence. But most experts agree that children are able to understand and respond to the different demands of different relationships. If grandparents are only occasional baby-sitters, they should be allowed to make rules in their own home, although the parents may want to set some limits (on food, or bedtime, for instance). When the child returns, often all the parent has to say is, "I know Grandma lets you watch television in the afternoon, and when you go back to her house you can do it again. But at our house we have a different rule."

As care givers or frequent visitors in their grandchildren's home, however, grandparents should defer to the parents on child-rearing issues. By doing so, they are more likely to be consulted by the parents about their concerns than if they offer unsolicited advice. The most common conflict that arises between parents and grandparents is that the parents feel they are being criticized or second-guessed. Because attitudes toward discipline have changed over the last few decades, this can be a particularly touchy subject for parents and grandparents.

Before enlisting a grandparent as a care giver, it is important to bring these issues into the open and not to assume that you will agree. Even if you had a happy childhood and get along well now, your mother may have different memories. In a recent study, for example, the grandmothers remembered putting little emphasis on teaching their young children. Their daughters, however, remembered this teaching as a focus of their early life. Certainly these daughters might be disappointed in their expectations of their mothers as care givers for their own children.

Discuss with your parent or in-law his or her philosophy of child-rearing if you have never done so before. Talk about discipline. Talk about how you were raised. If you have uncomfortable memories from your childhood, this is the time to air them. Watch her with your children. Finally, consider your own relationship. Beware the grandparent who still treats you or your spouse like a child, taking the attitude that grandma or grandpa knows best and ignoring your wishes about how to handle your children.

Baby-Sitters

It is possible to put the same kind of effort into selecting an occasional nighttime baby-sitter as into selecting a full-time care giver—but few parents do. The time-consuming process would have to be repeated over and over as temporary sitters graduate, move, or get full-time jobs.

Many parents settle instead for a meeting beforehand to introduce the children and conduct a general discussion of problems to expect and of how things are handled in the family. In discussing discipline with a temporary baby-sitter, recommend measures less strict than those you might apply yourself. The words and actions of a stranger are not tempered by love, as yours would be. To prevent a misunderstanding, it is helpful to set ground rules for the evening with the baby-sitter in the presence of your children.

Parents are often tempted to employ their oldest child as a baby-sitter, with or without pay. This can be a good experience for the children, but there are also dangers parents should not overlook. According to Adele Faber, coauthor of *Siblings without Rivalry*, many adults are still angry at having been forced into the caretaker role as children. "The minute my sister was born," one woman told her, "I became her surrogate mother. I have always resented it. I felt she took away my childhood. To this day, my sister still expects the same relationship, and I want none of it."

Faber recommends that parents ask themselves several questions before recruiting an older sibling to babysit:

- Does the child want to baby-sit? She may say, "No, I'd rather be with my friends." Unless this is an emergency, the parent's response should be, "Fine." "If baby-sitting isn't voluntary," Faber says, "the resentment that spills over may harm the sibling."
- What kind of relationship do the children have? If an older sister is always teasing her younger brother, it would be bad for both of them to put her in charge. If the younger child seems upset to be put in her older sibling's care, take her unease seriously and try to find out *why* the child is upset. Sadly, some older siblings use their baby-sitting time to physically, verbally, or sexually abuse their younger brothers or sisters.

  With siblings who are close in age, Faber recommends not making the older one the boss. A mother could lay out some rules and state what she expects them to do while she is gone, and then say, "I'm putting each of you in charge of yourself."
- How responsible is the older child? Although this depends greatly on the individual child, rarely is an eight or nine year old experienced enough to handle an emergency situation. In any case, before giving the older

DISCIPLINE IN SPECIAL SITUATIONS

sibling a full-fledged baby-sitting job, Faber recommends a brief trial run.

One great advantage of sibling baby-sitters is that they know the ways of their younger brothers and sisters intimately and are familiar with the family's style for handling various situations. When the four year old balks at bedtime, her sister can counter confidently with, ''You know Mom always says one bedtime story, and then maybe one more if you're not tired. So let's go—which is the one you choose tonight?''

School and Beyond

As children grow up, they will encounter many situations in which they have to accept different styles of discipline. Schools, for instance, need to be safe and orderly (in most cases, more orderly than children's homes) so that children can learn. Different teachers create that environment in different ways. Some classrooms buzz; others are quiet. Children who have learned self-discipline and who bring to school a respect for the teacher and a respect for the work, should have no trouble adjusting. As the National PTA states in one of its publications, ''The discipline that children learn at home is the foundation for their behavior at school.''

Of course, no institution is perfect, and individual children have individual problems. When parents leave their children in the hands of others—care givers, camp counselors, or teachers—they still need to be watchful of the child's response. Although the child may not always verbalize the problem, she will generally offer some kind of cue that all is not okay.

CHAPTER FOURTEEN

· · · · · ·

Special Rules for Crises

Sickness, death, and divorce—these are all common crises that can strike any family. When a family is in crisis, discipline issues become more sensitive and complicated.

According to Dr. Ladd Spiegel, clinical instructor in the departments of psychiatry and psychiatry in pediatrics at Cornell University Medical College and psychiatrist for the Pediatric AIDS Clinic at New York Hospital, children generally react to crises in two ways. Both of which can tend to look like a worsening of behavior. Some children may regress, returning temporarily to ways they behaved when they were younger. Others may become less flexible. For example, a child who was moving easily from a relaxed home to a stricter school might not be able to make that transition when he is dealing with the additional stress of knowing that his father is very ill. He might insist on taking off his shoes in school, for instance, because that is allowed at home.

Dr. Spiegel offers parents two general principles for managing children's behavior during a crisis. The first is to treat children going through a period of regression not according to their actual age, but according to the age they are behaving. The second principle is to be consistent. Children are frightened of change, so that the more the environment, the structure, and the rules can remain the same, the better.

If bedtime for a seven-year-old boy was always 8:30 p.m.,

then it should still be 8:30 p.m. when his father moves out following a divorce, for example. On the other hand, if he refuses to go to bed and acts babyish in other ways, his mother should try to remember how she handled bedtime a few years back. Rather than reason with him, explaining that he will be tired the next day, she might sit at the foot of his bed for a while or put on a night-light. In the morning, however, the child should be expected to get up and get dressed himself, as he always does. "Parents and caretakers want to allow the regression," according to Dr. Spiegel, "and encourage a rapid recovery."

Each kind of crisis, however, has special dimensions of its own. When children are physically ill, especially if they are hospitalized, the parents share their care with doctors and nurses. They no longer have control over what their children eat, when they go to sleep, or what they wear. Yet it is still important for them to keep consistent whatever they can. Some physically ill children express their anger by swearing, for instance, and parents can insist that the old rules about such language apply. Meanwhile, they must help their child deal with the anger he is feeling concerning his illness and/or hospitalization. Parents can also meet with the hospital staff to come up with a new set of rules for the new situation.

With a sick or hospitalized child, Dr. Spiegel says, a parent might want to err in the direction of being too strict. "A child who is in the hospital is very frightened by the new environment and needs very clear rules in order to deal with the anxiety." With a child whose *parent* is sick or dying, however, a parent would want to err in the other direction. "In general, that child will experience guilt, imagine that he or she has contributed to the parent's illness or death. Rules that are too severe or punishments that are too harsh may be interpreted by the child as punishment for the imagined crime of having hurt the parent.''

In the beginning of a divorce, as with some other crises, parents sometimes try to protect their children from the truth. This approach, according to Dr. Spiegel, often backfires. ''Being excluded from discussions and from the knowledge of it, the child is going to make demands for attention and inclusion, and the child is going to make those demands in behavior, not in words.''

In a crisis, parents, too, tend to regress and become less flexible, so that they are less able to behave in an understanding, creative way with their children. According to Drs. Wallerstein and Kelly in *Surviving the Breakup,* ''Setting appropriate routines and formulating rules for the new family unit were among the more difficult tasks for women newly cast as head of the family.''

During a crisis, Dr. Spiegel recommends that parents spend 15 or 20 minutes a day trying to find out what is going on in their children's lives. ''Parents who don't normally have to set a time aside to talk to their children, but just do it because they are aware, may have to make this new structure for themselves.'' Although some parents may be tempted to send their children to a relative or a babysitter during a crisis, Dr. Spiegel suggests that the parents get help for themselves instead, whether it be from a cleaning person, who can relieve them of some of the day-to-day workload, or a psychotherapist with whom they can discuss positive ways of responding to a negative situation. ''There is no one as good for the child in a crisis as the parent.''

Once the crisis is over, parents may find that their children have developed some undesirable behaviors. The best response is to return the family to normal as quickly as possible. "Now it's time to get back to the way we always did things," the parent might say. "Generally kids are so relieved by that," says Dr. Spiegel, "the results are almost instantaneous."

Afterword
Teaching by Example

• • • • • •

"Clean up your room immediately!" a mother yells to her six year old from a perch on her own unmade bed littered with the last week's newspapers and the remains of an afternoon snack. "Silence!" shrieks a father. Or he yells, "Stop hitting your brother!" as he smacks his eight year old on the behind.

All parents are occasionally guilty of giving their children mixed messages, asking them to "do as I say, not as I do." Occasionally this is all right, so long as when confronted with the inconsistency, you admit your mistake. ("Oops, you're right. I guess we'd better both straighten our rooms. And then let's give ourselves a treat," the mother of the six year old might say.) Parents who can admit their mistakes show strength, not weakness. They also teach their children how to back down with honor from positions they may regret.

Similarly, a parent who smokes cigarettes can still warn her children about the dangers of smoking. She can explain that this is a difficult habit to break, although she is trying, and can enlist their support. This model may even make it easier for them to ask for help with their problems.

197

Making and Breaking Rules

In general, parents should try hard to practice what they preach. According to Dr. Michael Schulman and Eva Mekler, authors of *Bringing Up a Moral Child*, "Children learn from observing. . . . If you preach goodness to your child but he sees that you don't practice it, the research evidence suggests that he will be more influenced by what you do than by what you say. As he gets older, he's also likely to resent you for being a hypocrite."

Discipline is one way parents teach their children values. If generosity is a value of yours, you will probably encourage your children, when they are old enough, to share their toys and give away those they have outgrown. They will also see you being generous to your friends and relatives and to the people who work for you. They may remember the pleasure with which you lent your sister a skirt when they are asked to do something similar. If politeness is one of your values, you will probably expect your children to say "please" and "thank you." And they will see you greeting the bus driver in the morning, thanking the waitress when she delivers your meal, and thanking your children, too, when they run back to the house to fetch something you forgot.

Every rule you make reflects your values, but so does every rule you break. "Television has never been a problem for us," one mother says. "My husband and I watch only rarely—special shows—and that is all the kids expect to do. But food is another matter. We both eat sweets and drink soda. We tried not to let our children do it, but it didn't work. I suppose we didn't care enough. If we had, we would have changed our own eating habits."

Before you make family rules, it is worthwhile to spend

some time identifying the values to which you are most committed, those which you will endorse with your own behavior. What you do only halfheartedly, your children will do only halfheartedly too, whether it is eating nutritious food or participating in religious observance. One parent remembers overhearing tales of her father's stay at a health spa, where he regularly sneaked out at night for steak and potatoes. No wonder she never took his lectures on nutrition very seriously. And many nonobservant adults remember being dropped off at religious school by parents who otherwise never set foot inside the church or synagogue.

All the same rules, of course, do not apply equally to parents and children. But the same underlying principles should. Just because your preteen has an eight o'clock curfew does not mean that you have to be home by eight o'clock, too. On the other hand, many parents who impose curfews do so out of concern for their children's safety. Having described some of the late-night dangers, they should respect their children's concern for adults' safety as well. They should leave a number where they can be reached when they are out and an estimated time of return, and then call if they will be later.

The Medium Is the Message

You teach your children values not only through the rules you choose to make, but also through the ways you enforce them. "Why do I have to take a bath?" a child might whine. If her father answers, "Because I say so," the most obvious lesson is that "might is right."

Another parent might answer, "Because keeping your

body clean is one way to stay healthy. But I know your favorite television show starts soon, so let me help you get it done quickly.'' This parent is giving reasons to support the rule that children should take regular baths, as well as understanding and respecting the child's own conflicting interests.

Parents who explain and reason with their children reap the reward of cooperative behavior, or at least of reasoning, in return. They are also equipping their children with a valuable skill for getting along in the world.

Children who are allowed to take part in setting rules learn several more lessons. They learn that there may be many different points of view on a single issue, based on personal preferences and that all of them deserve a hearing. They learn how important it is to compromise in order to reach an agreement. They also learn from watching their parents how to negotiate effectively.

One parent might respond to a sibling squabble with: ''You should love your baby sister, not fight with her.'' Another parent might say, ''The baby is really making you angry by getting into your things, isn't she? I can't let you hit her, but let's put this stuff out of her reach.'' The second parent is acknowledging rather than denying the child's feelings. She is also teaching her that there are effective ways to resolve problems without resorting to violence.

Parents who use spankings as their sole means of discipline, on the other hand, are teaching their children to use force to settle disputes. They should not be surprised when their children use this same force on their friends and siblings.

The Best Teachers

There are many ways in which parents try to help their children become good human beings. But there is one lesson in particular that you can teach better than anyone else—how to be a good parent. After all, there are no other models children will ever study so closely or for so long. One mother, complimented on how well she was raising her children, answered with the words every parent must secretly yearn to hear one day: "Anything I do right with my children, I learned from my mother."

Resources

• • • • • •

Books for Adults

Ames, Louise B. *He Hit Me First: When Brothers and Sisters Fight.* New York: Dembner Books, 1983.
   Tips on how to diminish parent involvement in sibling disagreements.

Balter, Dr. Lawrence. *Dr. Balter's Child Sense: Understanding and Handling the Common Problems of Infancy and Early Childhood.* New York: Poseidon Press, 1985.
   Practical, common sense and specific advice on child rearing. Self-discipline is the goal of discipline according to this well-respected child psychologist.

Balter, Dr. Lawrence, with Anita Shreve. *Who's in Control: Dr. Balter's Guide to Discipline Without Combat.* New York: Poseidon Press/Simon & Schuster, 1989.
   How to direct your children, set an example, anticipate, distract and intervene without losing control and lashing out. Written by well-known child psychologist and television personality.

Berenstain, Stan and Jan. *The Berenstains' Baby Book.* New York: Arbor House, 1983.
   Successful children's book authors and survivors of the "parent wars," the Berenstains offer practical advice on parenting. Humorous.

Bettelheim, Bruno. *A Good Enough Parent: A Book on Child-Rearing.* New York: Knopf, 1987.

Not another how-to book, but a dense, rich, reflective, intuitive, psychoanalytical work on the parent-child relationship by a preeminent child psychologist. Compassionate and inspirational. Bettelheim advises parents to resist the impulse to create the child they would like to have, instead help the child to develop fully into the person the child wishes to and can fruitfully become.

Bramnick, Lea, and Anita Simon. *The Parents' Solution Book: Your Child from Five to Twelve.* New York: Watts, 1983.
Practical handbook with tips, hints, activities, and sample dialogue to cover a wide range of everyday situations. Emphasis is on preventing problems.

Brazelton, T. Berry. *Toddlers and Parents.* New York: Delacorte, 1974.
Delightful and penetrating look at children's early years through profiles and anecdotes. A variety of behaviors and other issues are examined by this distinguished pediatrician.

Brazelton, T. Berry. *What Every Baby Knows.* Reading, MA: Addison-Wesley, 1987.
Verbatim dialogue and commentary provide insights into childhood problems and issues.

Brenner, Barbara. *Love and Discipline.* New York: Ballantine, 1983.
Reassuring guidelines to help parents discover what works best for their particular child. One of the Bank Street College of Education Child Development Series. Available in hardcover and paperback.

Brett, Doris. *Annie Stories.* New York: Workman, 1986.
Nine stories to help children cope with emotions and anxieties of childhood situations such as nightmares, birth of siblings, and starting school. The author, a clinical psychologist, tells parents how to adapt stories to the needs of their own child. Insightful. Paperback.

Briggs, Dorothy Corkille. *Your Child's Self-Esteem: Step-By-Step Guidelines for Raising Responsible, Productive, Happy Children.* Garden City, New York: Dolphin/Doubleday, 1970.
Discusses the importance of self-esteem to healthy emotional

development and gives practical advice on how to help create strong feelings of self-worth in your child.

Burns, Cherie. *Stepmotherhood: How to Survive Without Feeling Frustrated, Left Out, or Wicked.* New York: Harper & Row, 1985.
Stepmother Cherie Burns gives frank, insightful and practical advice on stepmothering. She has interviewed stepmothers across the country and consulted with family counselors, covering everything from ex-wives, visitation schedules, money, vacation, sex, guilt, discipline, and housework.

Calladine, Andrew and Carole. *Raising Brothers and Sisters without Raising the Roof.* Minneapolis, MN: Winston Press, 1983.
Practical, straightforward advice.

Canter, Lee, with Marlene Canter. *Assertive Discipline.* New York: Perennial Library/Harper & Row, 1985.
Assertiveness-training manual for parents. Emphasis on communications skills. Revised edition published in 1988.

Chess, Stella, M.D., and Thomas Alexander. M.D. *Know Your Child: An Authoritative Guide for Today's Parents.* New York: Basic Books, 1987.
Two renowned psychiatrists offer reassuring wisdom and solid, practical information based on thirty years of research. They cover most important issues, including temperament and its significance, sibling rivalry, separation anxiety, early schooling, and adolescent rebellion.

Clark, Lynn, Ph.D. *Time-Out Solution: A Parent's Guide for Handling Everyday Behavior Problems.* Chicago: Contemporary Books, 1989.
How to replace your child's bad behavior with good behavior and help your child to achieve self-discipline. A positive approach to discipline, explained in a practical, step-by-step manner.

Crary, Elizabeth. *Without Spanking or Spoiling: A Practical Approach to Toddler and Preschool Guidance.* Seattle, WA: Parenting Press, 1979.
A practical guide to teaching children to cooperate and problem solve. Paperback, reprinted in 1988.

Dinkmeyer, Don, and Gary D. McKay, *The Parent's Handbook: Systematic Training for Effective Parenting (STEP)*. Circle Pines, MN: American Guidance Service/Random House, 1982.

This workbook format aids parents to develop their child's sense of responsibility, cooperation, self-reliance and mutual respect between parent and child.

Dinkmeyer, Don, and Gary D. McKay. *Raising a Responsible Child: Practical Steps to Successful Family Relationships*. New York: Simon & Schuster, 1973.

Specific, family-centered egalitarian methods of discipline to benefit the entire family and to create a healthful environment for growth.

Dodson, Fitzhugh. *How to Discipline with Love: From Crib to College*. New York: Rawson, 1977.

Comprehensive, eclectic guide with emphasis on developmental appropriateness and the uniqueness of each child and situation. Includes advice for single and stepparents.

Dunn, Judy. *Sisters and Brothers*. Cambridge, MA: Harvard University Press, 1985.

Why do some siblings get along harmoniously and affectionately, while others constantly squabble? To what extent are parents responsible for differences in siblings' personalities? How can parents ease tensions? Another in the Developing Child series, this book is based on new research and gives a fresh perception of one of the most crucial and long-lasting relationships people can have. Includes practical advice on coping. Paperback.

Einstein, Elizabeth. *The Stepfamily: Living, Loving & Learning*. Boston: Shambhala, 1985 (originally published in 1982 by Macmillan).

Information and advice on how to keep "blended families" together and realize their potential for happiness and fulfillment. A sensitive exploration of the difficulties to be faced and the ways to overcome them, written by a woman who is both a stepdaughter and stepmother. Paperback.

Elkind, David. *Miseducation: Preschoolers at Risk*. New York: Knopf, 1988.

Dr. Elkind discusses how early miseducation can cause permanent damage to a child's self-esteem and subsequent attitude to learning. He warns against the pressures to try to raise a "superkid." An important and compassionate book by one of the most respected names in the field of early childhood education.

Ephron, Delia. *Funny Sauce: Us, the Ex, the Ex's New Mate, the Mate's Ex, and the Kids.* New York: Viking, 1986.

The author of *How to Eat Like a Child* and *Teenage Romance* has turned her pen to the new American family. Hilarious, wise, comic and insightful, Ms. Ephron shares stories about her husband and two stepchildren.

Faber, Adele, and Elaine Mazlish. *How to Talk So Kids Will Listen and Listen So Kids Will Talk.* New York: Rawson, Wade, 1980.

Effective, supportive method of enlisting child's cooperation in solving problems. Based on the work of child psychologist Haim Ginott. Also available as an Avon paperback.

Faber, Adele, and Elaine Mazlish. *Siblings without Rivalry: How to Help Your Children Live Together So You Can Live Too.* New York: Avon, 1988.

Humor, compassion, understanding and practical advice, based on the principles of child psychologist Haim Ginott.

Ferber, Richard, M.D. *Solve Your Child's Sleep Problems.* New York: Fireside/Simon & Schuster, 1985.

How to help your child fall and stay asleep. Tips, suggestions, sample problems and solutions plus a bibliography of children's "go-to-sleep" books by the Director of the Center for Pediatric Sleep Disorders, Children's Hospital, Boston.

Fleming, Don, with Linda Balahoutis. *How to Stop the Battle with Your Child: A Practical Guide to Solving Everyday Problems with Children.* New York: Prentice Hall Press, 1987.

Real-life situations presented with reasonable solutions that include identifying reasonable parental expectations along with graduated suggestions for coping in case the first idea doesn't work. Emphasis on understanding your child's motives, feelings, and abilities. Paperback.

Fraiberg, Selma H. *The Magic Years: Understanding and Handling the Problems of Early Childhood.* New York: Charles Scribner's Sons, 1959.

The inner workings of the mind and emotions of children from birth to six years are described with warmth and perception. Provides insight into dealing with issues of discipline and self-control. Available in hardcover and paperback.

Ginott, Haim G. *Between Parent and Child.* New York: Macmillan, 1965.

Emphasizes the need for skillful, caring communication with children. Written with compassion and humor by the late renowned child psychologist. Available in hardcover and paperback.

Gordon, Thomas. *P.E.T. Parent Effectivenss Training: The Tested Way to Raise Responsible Children.* New York: New American Library, 1970.

A structured method of open-ended dialoguing and discussion to promote less fighting, fewer tantrums, closer and warmer relationships, and more responsbile children. Available in hardcover and paperback.

Guarendi, Raymond N. *You're a Better Parent Than You Think!: A Guide to Common-Sense Parenting.* Englewood Cliffs, NJ: Prentice Hall, 1985.

Debunks popular myths of parenting, including the need to be perfect. Emphasizes practical, commonsense approaches and encourages parents to trust themselves as it tries to guide them through the maze of professional jargon. Discusses, for example, what is normal. Available in hardcover and paperback.

Hirschmann, Jane R., and Lela Zaphiropoulos. *Are You Hungry?: A Completely New Approach to Raising Children Free of Food and Weight Problems.* New York: Signet/New American Library, 1985.

A revolutionary program for creating lifelong patterns of healthful self-demand eating. Addresses misconceptions about nutrition such as the myth of the balanced meal. Through case studies and anecdotes these two experts in eating disorders offer a way to demystify food, prevent future problems and make mealtimes a pleasure. Paperback.

Isaacs, Susan. *Who's in Control: A Parent's Guide to Discipline.* New York: Perigee/Putnam, 1986.

What to do to change your discipline style to make it more effective and efficient. Paperback.

Kavanaugh, Dorriet, *Listen To Us! The Children's Express Report.* New York: Workman, 1978.

Children, ages six to 13, speak out about parents, siblings, friends, sex, school, responsiblities, and happiness. Edited from roundtable discussions among more than 2,000 children. Available in hardcover and paperback.

Kelly, Jeffrey. *Solving Your Child's Behavior Problems: An Everyday Guide for Parents.* Boston: Little, Brown, 1983.

Focuses on behavior problems of children ages three to six. Although academic in tone, it does provide practical suggestions. By a clincial psychologist.

Keshet, Jamie K. *Love and Power in the Stepfamily: A Practical Guide.* New York: McGraw-Hill, 1987.

Advice and strategies by a family therapist who specializes in working with blended families.

Klein, Carole. *How It Feels to Be a Child.* New York: Harper & Row, 1975.

The importance of recognizing and accepting the painful feelings of childhood. Compassionate and perceptive. Originally titled *The Myth of the Happy Child.* Paperback.

Lansky, Vicki. *Practical Parenting Tips.* Deephaven, MN: Meadowbrook Press, 1980.

Over 1,000 parent-tested ideas on everything from discipline to sibling rivalry. Wit, compassion, and common sense.

Lansky, Vicki. *Practical Parenting Tips for the School-Age Years.* New York: Bantam, 1985.

More excellent advice for parents of children in elementary school.

LeShan, Eda. *When Your Child Drives You Crazy.* New York: St. Martin's Press, 1985.

Warm, personal, practical advice on raising children from toddlers to teens. How to "read" behavior and identify hidden agendas.

Lickona, Thomas. *Raising Good Children: Helping Your Child through the Stages of Moral Development*. New York: Bantam, 1983.

Practical advice, real-life examples of how to handle discipline issues to instill honesty, courtesy, helpfulness, and respect for others. Discusses research and explains stages of moral development.

Mason, Diane, Gayle Jensen, and Carolyn Ryzewicz. *No More Tantrums . . . and Other Good News*. Chicago: Contemporary Books, 1987.

Lighthearted, reassuring handbook that covers everyday problems from sandbox violence to messy rooms and sharing to tattling. Practical, sound advice. Paperback.

Miller, Alice. *For Your Own Good: Hidden Cruelty in Childrearing and the Roots of Violence*. New York: Frarrar, Straus & Giroux, 1983.

Translated from the German, this ground-breaking study of the origins of violence is shattering, frightening, convincing, illuminating and thought-provoking. It focuses on the idea of punishing our children for the painful actions of our parents in a form of "repetition compulsion." Miller stresses the need to acknowlege childhood sufferings "lest we pass them on unconsciously to the next generation." Written in a clear, engaging style.

Reit, Seymour V. *Sibling Rivalry*. New York: Ballantine, 1985.

Practical guide on what to expect and options for coping. One of the excellent Bank Street College of Education Series. A sensitive, sensible approach. Paperback.

Rogers, Fred, and Barry Head. *Mister Rogers Talks with Parents*. New York: Berkeley, 1983.

How to cope with everyday problems and make family life and child rearing as rewarding as possible by televison's respected expert on children. Compassionate, commonsense approach. Paperback.

Rubin, Theodore Isaac, M.D. *The Angry Book*. New York: Collier/Macmillan, 1969.

How to make friends with your anger and really take charge of your emotions. Dr. Rubin, eminent psychiatrist and writer, reminds us that suppressed or twisted anger can lead to anxiety, depression, misery and more. He provides helpful advice on how not to be afraid of anger—your own and others'. Paperback.

Samalin, Nancy, with Martha Moraghan Jablow. *Loving Your Child Is Not Enough: Positive Discipline That Works.* New York: Viking, 1987.

Emphasizes the "need to be permissive with children's feelings, yet strict about their behavior." Explicit, practical advice as well as overall philosophy promoting ways of improved communication with children.

Sanger, Sirgay, M.D., and John Kelly. *The Woman Who Works, the Parent Who Cares: A Revolutionary Program for Raising Your Child.* New York: Perennial Library/Harper & Row, 1987.

How to encourage the development of a more self-confident, independent and socially skilled child and meet the competing demands of work and motherhood.

Sanger, Sirgay, M.D., and John Kelly. *You and Your Baby's First Year.* New York: Bantam, 1987.

Based on Dr. Sanger's research in infant development, this book focuses on the subtle baby/parent interaction—how to "read" your infant's cues—and the development of the "wondrous dance of communication" between parents and child to foster a magical bond that will help your infant grow mentally, physically and emotionally.

Savage, Karen, and Patricia Adams. *The Good Stepmother: A Practical Guide.* New York: Crown, 1988.

Covers everything from money, sex, the ex-wife, and the stages that stepfamilies go through from courtship onward. An anecdotal approach which helps stepparents to identify with and learn from familiar situations.

Schulman, Michael, and Eva Mekler. *Bringing Up a Moral Child: A New Approach for Teaching Your Child to Be Kind, Just, and Responsible.* Reading, MA: Addison-Wesley, 1985.

Sound, research-based how-to manual that not only advises,

but explains moral development and the growth of conscience. Available in hardcover and paperback.

Sears, William. *The Fussy Baby: How to Bring Out the Best in Your High-Need Child.* New York: New American Library, 1985.
Sensitive advice on how to soothe and nurture a high-need child from infant to toddler. A La Leche League International book. Paperback.

Silberman, Melvin, and Susan W. Wheelan. *How to Discipline without Feeling Guilty: Assertive Relationships with Children.* New York: Hawthorn Books, 1980.
Defining limits and helping children to observe them.

Smith, Manuel J. *Yes, I Can Say No: A Parent's Guide to Assertiveness Training for Children.* New York: Arbor House, 1986.
Step-by-step program to help parents teach their children to cope with assertiveness issues such as bullies, criticism, mistakes, and peer pressure.

Spock, Benjamin. *Raising Children in a Difficult Time.* New York: Pocket Books/Simon & Schuster, 1976.
Reassuring common sense to see parents and children through the difficulties of living in the modern world by the man who wrote the book on baby care.

Spock, Benjamin, and Michael Rothenberg. *Dr. Spock's Baby and Child Care.* New York: Pocket Books/Simon & Schuster, 1985.
The classic child-rearing manual. Comprehensive, reliable information about the physical and emotional health of children. Paperback (revised edition).

Turecki, Stanley, and Leslie Tonner. *The Difficult Child.* New York: Bantam, 1985.
Step-by-step approach to understanding and managing hard-to-raise children. Compassionate, nonjudgmental approach.

Wallerstein, Judith S., and Joan Berlin Kelly. *Surviving the Breakup: How Children and Parents Cope with Divorce.* New York: Basic Books, 1980.
This important study explores and documents the immediate and long-range effects of divorce on children. The findings

strongly suggest the need to rethink the entire process and consider ways to minimize some of the harmful effects on children. Paperback.

White, Burton L. *The First Three Years of Life.* rev. ed. Englewood Cliffs, NJ: Prentice Hall, 1985.

Author describes in detail the physical, emotional, and mental development of the young child. He emphasizes the importance of the first three years to lifelong learning. A classic. Available in hardcover and paperback.

White, Burton L. *Educating the Infant and Toddler.* Lexington, MA: Lexington Books, 1988.

Reliable, practical information on what is and is not known about the learning process and developmental stages of young children by the renowned researcher. Authoritative and readable. Available in hardcover and paperback.

Wyckoff, Jerry, and Barbara C. Unell. *Discipline without Shouting or Spanking: Practical Solutions to the Most Common Preschool Behavior Problems.* New York: Meadowbrook Books/Simon & Schuster, 1984.

Effective, practical, nonviolent options for coping with preschool behavioral issues. Easy-to-use manual arrangement. Available in hardcover and paperback.

Books for Children

Alexander, Martha. *Move Over, Twerp.* New York: Dial, 1981.

Jeffery finds a way to stand up for himself and stop being bullied by the bigger kids. For ages 4-7.

Aliki. *Feelings.* New York: Greenwillow, 1984.

Various emotions are portrayed in pictures, dialogue, stories, and poems. Helps children identify and talk about their feelings. For ages 5-9. Available in hardcover and paperback.

RESOURCES

Ancona, George. *Helping Out*. New York: Clarion, 1985.

An exploration, in black-and-white photographs, of the pleasure and special relationships of adults and children working together.

Balter, Dr. Lawrence. *What's the Matter with A.J.?: Understanding Jealousy*. New York: Barron's, 1989.

A.J. is having a hard time adjusting to the arrival of his new baby sister. A caring teacher and friend offer him advice. But it is Mom and Dad who finally help him resolve his feelings. The story is enclosed between two short discussions of this problem by Dr. Balter to further aid parents and teachers in dealing with sibling jealousy. For ages 4-7.

Berenstain, Stan and Jan. *The Berenstain Bears Forget Their Manners*. New York: Random House, 1985.

Mama Bear comes up with a plan to correct the Bear family's rude behavior. For ages 3-8. Available in hardcover and paperback.

Berenstain, Stan and Jan. *The Berenstain Bears Get the Gimmies*. New York: Random House, 1988.

Gran and Gramps Bear come up with a plan to rid the cubs of their greediness. For ages 3-8. Available in hardcover and paperback.

Berenstain, Stan and Jan. *The Berenstain Bears Get in a Fight*. New York: Random House, 1988.

Sibling rivalry is examined in this playful, but insightful series about the Bear family. For ages 3-8. Available in hardcover and paperback.

Brown, Marc, and Stephen Krensky. *Perfect Pigs: An Introduction to Manners*. Boston: Atlantic Monthly/Little, Brown, 1983.

Funny, engaging, and simple introduction to good manners for all occasions including meals, parties, telephone conversations and interactions with family, friends, and pets. For ages 4-8. Available in hardcover and paperback.

Burns, Marilyn. *I Am Not a Short Adult!: Getting Good at Being a Kid*. Boston: Little, Brown, 1977.

Parents, siblings, responsibility, television, school, and how to decide for yourself what kind of kid you want to be. For ages 9-12. Available in hardcover and paperback.

Galdone, Paul. *The Little Red Hen.* New York: Clarion, 1973.
Familiar nursery classic about responsibility and sharing in the rewards of labor. For ages 3-5. Available in hardcover and paperback.

Gauch, Patricia Lee. *Christina Katerina and the Time She Quit the Family.* Illustrated by Elise Primavera. New York: Putnam, 1987.
Unhappy with the way her family is treating her, Christina Katerina decides to quit them and strike out on her own. She stays at home, but changes her name and the rules of the game. Irrepressible heroine who learns a lesson in family relationships. For ages 4-8.

Gretz, Susanna. *Roger Loses His Marbles.* New York: Dial, 1988.
Unhappy because he has lost his favorite marbles and because he must clean his room for Aunt Lulu's visit, Roger, a young pig, turns sulky. Clever Aunt Lulu finds a way to help Roger out of the sulks. For ages 3-7.

Hapgood, Miranda. *Martha's Mad Day.* Illustrated by Emily McCully. New York: Crown, 1977.
It takes Martha the whole day to work out her angry feelings. For ages 3-6.

Hickman, Martha Whitmore. *Good Manners for Girls and Boys.* Photographs by Nancy Harris Blackwelder. New York: Crown, 1985.
Children show how good manners and consideration for others make for better times in a variety of situations. Illustrated with color photographs of culturally and ethnically diverse children. For ages 4-6.

Joslin, Sesyle. *What Do You Do, Dear?* Illustrated by Maurice Sendak. New York: Harper & Row, 1961.
Sequel to honor-winning *What Do You Say, Dear?* this humorous title stimulates discussion and reflection on proper behavior through exaggeration and nonsense. Good fun. For ages 4-8. Available in hardcover and paperback.

Kalb, Jonah, and David Viscott. *What Every Kid Should Know.* Boston: Houghton Mifflin, 1976.

Reassuring look at feelings. The emphasis is on understanding yourself and how to get along with others, including parents. For ages 9-12.

Keats, Ezra Jack. *Peter's Chair.* New York: Harper & Row, 1967.

It takes Peter a while to adjust to the idea of a baby-sister. A classic. For ages 3-6. Available in hardcover and paperback.

Kraus, Robert. *Herman the Helper.* Illustrated by Jose Aruego and Ariane Dewey. New York: Prentice Hall, 1974.

The pleasures of helping others is demonstrated in this colorfully illustrated story of a friendly octopus. For ages 2-5. Available in hardcover and paperback.

Kraus, Robert. *Boris Bad Enough.* Illustrated by Jose Aruego. New York: Simon & Schuster, 1976.

Boris' parents take him to a psychiatrist when his behavior continues to get worse and worse. The psychiatrist has some advice for the whole elephant family. For ages 3-6. Available in hardcover and paperback.

Lobel, Arnold. *Frog and Toad Are Friends.* New York: Harper & Row, 1970.

Childhood classic about friendship, written and illustrated with warmth, wisdom, and humor. For ages 3-8. Available in hardcover and paperback.

Potter, Beatrix. *The Tale of Peter Rabbit.* London: Frederick Warne, 1902.

Childhood classic of a naughty bunny who misbehaves and is punished. Warm, wonderful, and reassuring. For ages 3-5. Reprinted in 1987.

Rogers, Fred. *Making Friends.* Photographs by Jim Judkis. New York: Putnam, 1987.

Mr. Rogers explains what it means to be a friend and some of the difficulties and special rewards of friendship. For ages 2-6.

Rosen, Winifred. *Henrietta, The Wild Woman of Borneo.* Illustrated by Kay Chorao. New York: Four Winds, 1975.

When Henrietta, who can't seem to please anyone, is called the Wild Woman of Borneo, she decides to mail herself there. Funny and moving. For ages 4-8.

Ross, Tony. *The Boy Who Cried Wolf.* New York: Dial, 1985.

In this contemporary and droll retelling of the Aesop fable, Willy cries wolf to get out of taking a bath and practicing his violin, until the wolf really appears. For ages 4-8. Available in hardcover and paperback.

Sendak, Maurice. *Pierre: A Cautionary Tale in Five Chapters and a Prologue.* New York: Harper & Row, 1962.

The cautionary tale of a young boy who simply doesn't care, even when faced by a hungry lion. Droll and delightful through every rereading. For ages 3-8. Also available as part of The Nutshell Library.

Sendak, Maurice. *Where the Wild Things Are.* New York: Harper & Row, 1963.

Modern classic of childhood anger. Max is naughty and gets sent to bed without his supper. He resolves his feelings in a dream. Upon awakening he finds his supper waiting and still hot. Caldecott Medal winner by the modern master of children's books. For ages 3-7. Available in hardcover and paperback.

Seuss, Dr. *Horton Hatches the Egg.* New York: Random House, 1940.

About the elephant who is "faithful one hundred percent" who means what he says and says what he means. No better model of responsibility available. A classic and fun. For ages 4-8.

Steig, William. *Spinky Sulks.* New York: Farrar, Straus & Giroux, 1988.

Spinky is angry at his family and won't stop sulking, no matter what they do. A playful look at family relations, with appealing illustrations. For ages 3-8.

Steptoe. John. *Daddy Is a Monster . . . Sometimes.* New York: Lippincott, 1980.

Warm, humorous family story. Bweela and her brother Javaka think their Daddy is nice, but sometimes he turns into a scary monster. Daddy says, "Well, I'm probably a monster daddy when

I got monster kids.'' Reassuring, thought-provoking story about discipline and feelings. Written in a delicate black English. On target. For ages 4-7.

Udry, Janice May. *Let's Be Enemies.* Illustrated by Maurice Sendak. New York: Harper & Row, 1961.
    John and James go from friends to enemies and back again. For ages 3-7. Available in hardcover and paperback.

Zemach, Margoat. *It Could Always Be Worse.* New York: Farrar, Straus & Giroux, 1976.
    This Yiddish folk tale turns logic on its side when a poor man who lives with his mother, wife, and six children in a one-room house asks the rabbi for advice. The meaning of the title soon becomes clear. For ages 4+. Available in hardcover and paperback.

Zolotow, Charlotte. *The Quarreling Book.* Illustrated by Arnold Lobel. New York: Harper & Row, 1963.
    It is a rainy day and the entire James family feels cranky and quarrelsome. Hurt feelings are passed on from family member to family member until the dog, who responds playfully, reverses the situation. For ages 4-8. Available in hardcover and paperback.

Zolotow, Charlotte. *The Hating Book.* Illustrated by Ben Schecter. New York: Harper & Row, 1969.
    A little girl hates her friend, who won't sit next to her on the school bus. At her mother's prodding, she overcomes her anger and fear of rejection to talk things out with her friend. Deftly handled. For ages 3-7.

INDEX

• • • • • •

Defiance, 154
Dependency, 30
Depression, 120
Development
  differences in, 29
  of infants, 29–31
  of preschoolers, 35–36
  of preteens, 41–43
  of toddlers, 31–35
Dialogues, 83–84, 110
"Difficult" child
  definition of, 151–52
  discipline of
    and eye contact, 156
    ineffective, 153–54
    and overexcitement, 155–
      56
    professional help for, 158–
      59
    and rewards vs.
      punishments, 157
    and temperament, 154–55
    and transitions, 155
  parents of, 152–53
  temperament of, 23, 154–55
Discipline
  authoritative, 66–67
  and bodily functions, 46–50
  by care givers, 188–92
  constructive, 3, 13
  of "difficult" child. *See*
    "Difficult" child
  disagreement on, by parents
    benefits of, 136–37
    normality of, 131–32
    and past, 132–33

  problem solving of, 133–35
    and united front, 135–36
  and eating, 46, 48
  effective, 13–14, 112–13, 157
  and eliminating, 46–48
  by example, 197
  and good fit, 28
  ineffective, 153–54
  of infants, 30
  for listening, 77
  and love, 3
  permissive approach to, 4
  of preschoolers, 36
  of preteens, 46
  in single-parent families
    decision making in, 167–
      68
    new, 162–63
    pitfalls in, 163–65
    professional help for, 168–
      69
    responsibility in, 165–67
  and sleep, 46, 48
  in stepfamilies
    issue of, 172–73
    and normality, 178–79
    patience in, 173–76
    professional help for, 183–
      84
    rulemaking in, 176–77
  of toddlers, 31–32
Disobedience. *See* Misbehavior
Display of inadequacy, 112
Distractibility, 22
Divorce, 172, 177, 179–80, 195
Dressing routines, 39